CW00871776

A BRITISH RAJ
RAJ ATHWAL

Foreword copyright © John Sillett 2017
All other text and images copyright © Raj Athwal 2017

No part of the publication may be reproduced or copied, in print or in any
other form, expect for the purposes of review and/or criticism,
without the author's prior consent.

Typesetting by www.handebooks.co.uk

To my family, friends and all the dreamers in the world

CONTENTS

FOREWORD

People in football come and go, and some say we are ships in the night, but when you meet people who are doers not talkers they stay firmly etched in your mind, especially when they are achieving success in their field for your club.

Raj has certainly achieved major success for Coventry City, Watford and Glasgow Rangers and though admittedly his forward thinking, pro-active attitude and approach has been a major aspect in returning great results, I believe his ability to make everyone feel welcome and special is an equal attribute.

Certainly these traits were ingredients in his recognition when forwarded for his many awards.

When Raj joined Coventry City, he was one of the few who reignited my association with the great club with his enthusiasm and desire to make it a club people wanted to be at and enjoy visiting.

I can certainly say that he was a big reason for me enjoying my role as Club President and for that I will always be grateful.

In my mind his 'can do' spirit is one all clubs should embrace and I am sure with Arena Red he will be much sought after and enable a vehicle for continued success.

John Sillett

Coventry City Manager, 1986-1990
FA Cup winner 1987

INTRODUCTION

Hope, struggle, opportunity, racism, destiny, rejection; this book traces my life from humble working class roots in Coventry to overcoming adversity and fear to pursue my dreams. As a British born and bred Sikh of parents who emigrated from India, I am going to take you on an interesting, and hopefully inspiring, journey from growing up in the late 70s, where life appeared to be happy and care free, to the early 80s, where economic instability brought an ugly, intimidating culture to our streets. Being called a Paki and being chased by skinheads was part of growing up during a dark period. Trying to make sense of it all while embracing the music, football and opportunities my country would offer me added to the confusion as a teenager. There's a time for everything and, being an eternal optimist, I always believed in the future and the future did change for the better as a whole new world opened up, enabling me to pursue opportunities I could only dream of.

The complexities of accepting and integrating two cultures could be testing at the best of times. You grow up almost confused about your own identity and wanting to be accepted by everyone. From an early age you learn about disappointments and it's how you respond that can make or almost break you. Being told you are not good enough to go to University simply encouraged me to prove I had the ability. Begging for opportunities to earn a rightful living and being rejected time and time again made me even more determined to succeed, especially after one interview where I was blatantly told I was rejected because I was Asian. That was in 1994 not 1964!

The moment I walked into the Chairman's office at Coventry City Football Club, pleading for an opportunity, was the beginning of a journey taking in over 20 years behind the scenes in an industry alien to most of the world. An industry that has its own rules and regulations, a culture of its very own that is non-conventional, cut and thrust, yet intriguing and exciting to be part of. Coventry City Football Club gave me a chance in life. Watford Football Club changed me and allowed me to achieve a major milestone; while the mighty Glasgow Rangers made me and set me off on a journey I only ever dreamed of. Collectively these clubs gave me the confidence and temerity to challenge myself and deal with fear. Over time I realised fate and destiny are in our own hands. You can choose and create the life you want to live. There will always be obstacles and trials and tribulations, and from time to time we all screw up. That's life, accept it, move on and don't look back.

As my close friend Andy Moss once said to me, 'Everything you want or need is on the other side of fear'. How right he is. Overcome the emotion and you suddenly realise what you are capable of.

HOLBROOKS – WHERE IT ALL BEGAN

Born and raised in Coventry, I was from the North-West part of the city known as Holbrooks, bordering Whitmore Park, Foleshill and Radford. This was a predominantly Irish working class area. My early childhood memories are of playing about in the streets and on the green field opposite our house. I was always out with the local kids playing football or just hanging about. Growing up in the 70s was based on community spirit and people all knowing who your parents were. You never heard of paedophiles or were ever told by your parents to be careful of certain types of people. The general rule of thumb was never to speak to strangers.

Our house was located at Selworthy Road. We were lucky in that it was a three bedroom semi-detached with a garage. My father had bought the house for less than £2,000 in 1968. I remember him telling us several times how this was a monumental amount in those days. My parents had many opportunities to move to a more desirable area later on, but they were settled and knew most of the neighbours. This was a community after all.

Selworthy Road and Dunster Place were adjoined – one ventured into the next. In that vicinity alone we had some known characters and fantastic neighbours. Our immediate neighbours were the Springer family. They had originated from Barbados. As a kid growing up I was always in and out of their house. They treated me like their own and I got on really well with the lads, Mark and Richard, who were a few years older than me and their sisters, Jenny and Angela.

The other side of our house was the Robson family. They had moved into the area a few years before us and were a very well respected family. They had two kids,

Robert and Elizabeth, who were also a few years older than me. Their mother, Lucy, who was of Italian descent, got on very well with my mum and dad, which had as much to do with being foreigners as having similar values and culture. Lucy's husband, John, was a Geordie and always made time for our family. He knew the difficulties my mum and dad were experiencing during the 60s and always made a point of making sure all was fine with the family.

One of the fond memories I have of growing up is of John making me and my younger brother Sonny a cricket bat almost every summer from any piece of wood we could find. He knew we couldn't really afford a proper bat so ensured we had the best one in the area. John was also the only person to give me some money when I left for University. It was his way of saying you go and make a life for yourself.

The families on our street were from all over the world – it was almost like the United Nations. The summer months were great, as all the local kids would get together and we would either play football or rounders using the lampposts to get around. There were hardly any cars about, so you could play in the roads without worrying about hitting any vehicles. Most people didn't even worry about locking their front doors and, with the windows wide open, I was introduced to all types of music.

It was the Springer family who first introduced me to reggae music. The beat and melody was hypnotic. I couldn't make out the lyrics at this point; it was all about the melody. Looking back they had some excellent tunes from legendary artists such as Bob Marley, Gregory Isaac, Desmond Dekker, Dennis Brown and Jimmy Cliff. The vibe certainly resonated with the summer of 1976, when the country endured a heatwave. With all the social issues coming to the surface, music played a huge part in removing people from the reality they were living in. Music was a form of escapism from the harsh realities of life.

As the youngest among all the kids, I was looked after by the older kids, not that it mattered as I had this swagger about me and not a care in the world. It must have been the Jamaican influences. Growing up in the area as a youngster felt like an extended holiday. Always out playing or talking to the local kids, we were like one huge gang. Some nights there would often be fifteen to twenty kids playing about in the field or on the streets. There was never any trouble and all the parents knew all the kids.

It was during the mid to late 70s when it felt like someone had put the lights out. Overnight the country had descended into chaos and we were about to experience major social change to the infrastructure of the UK that reverberated for many years to come.

Even growing up in the late 70s and early 80s, when racism was an accepted part of daily life, I never had any real bother in our area. Having an older brother and his mates helped but for some reason I was always fine. It may also have a lot to do with the fact I had many friends from all backgrounds.

My earliest childhood memory is hanging about with one of my close pals at the time, Mark. We were literally inseparable as kids and certainly gave our parents a number of scares. Mark lived a few doors away in Dunster Place. Of similar age, we were always out together. If Mark was not at my house I would be in his. Both of us were from good, strict, working-class families. Unfortunately, many years later I discovered Mark had personal issues to contend with. The lad I knew was a jovial, happy-go-lucky character. After school, weekends or term time holidays it was always Mark and I. We were both extremely spirited kids and always up for a laugh.

One time we had the local constabulary out in force looking for us both. We decided to go to the local Holbrook Park to play on the swings and have a generally good time. The only problem was we were no older than 6 or 7. Unknown to us both our parents reported us to the local police as abducted. I do remember seeing a number of police cars scouring the area. When we decided to make our way back home, almost the whole street was out looking for us. We both could not understand the fuss. The look on my older brother's face said it all. My mum got hold of me in the street and gave me a few slaps on the backside. That was the only time she had ever laid a hand on me. The other times she could not catch me I was so quick. It was embarrassing having all these people staring at me, finger wagging that Mr Singh's son is going to be a problem when he grows up. To make matters worse, my dad had not returned from work so another round of beatings was awaiting me. Luckily my dad was on night shift so by the time I was up in the morning the anger of me going missing had passed away.

No matter what I did I would always end up in bother. My partner in crime was always Mark. Over from where we lived was a park/grassland area. It used to be a dog running track until the 60s. Now it was just open green land. Nearby was the storeroom for Unit Sales, a well known DIY company. As always, being bored during our holidays, we decided to have a closer look. We were probably no more than 8 or 9. The store reception was mostly unmanned and on impulse Mark decided to take some of the paint tubs while I was the lookout. It was harmless fun and we genuinely did not think anything of what we were doing other than having a laugh, as most kids did. I still remember Mark walking out with two tubs of paint almost the same size as him. In the end we just threw the tubs over by the railway tracks. Some people must have thought their luck was in when they found them unopened. That was until one day running out of the store with paint tubs in both hands we heard a shout. Looking back, a large man was making a dash for us. We both ran for it and every time I looked over my shoulder this man was getting closer. I could feel my heartbeat; how much further did we need to run? To make matters worse, Mark suffered from asthma, although that day he didn't seem to notice! The chaser got closer and closer until he suddenly tripped and fell over a rock and lay sprawling on the pavement. Not one to rejoice in someone's mishap, but this was like something out of the Benny Hill show. At this point I was out of breath and running on adrenaline. That had to be the quickest I had ever run and was soon to become my trademark. I was so scared as I thought he would call the police and Mark and I would end up in prison. That evening I spent the whole night looking out of my bedroom window waiting for the police to turn up. It's safe to say we never ventured near the Unit Sales DIY store on Lythalls Lane again.

My dad's brother lived around the corner from us in Dunster Place, which was always a problem for me. While I got on fantastically well with them, they always knew what I was up to as they lived a few doors from Mark's house. Everyone knew everyone's business. Importantly everyone looked out for each other. On one occasion I must have mentioned to Mark that my cousins were away for the day and that there was a box of marbles at the front door. The house actually had double patio doors with a small entrance. Mark and I decided to borrow the marbles and then put them back before my cousins arrived. We tried to make a small hole in the window but to no avail. Unfortunately the neighbours were watching and while we failed to take any marbles we left a crack in the window. Unbeknown to me the neighbours had explained everything to my uncle when he returned. Word got out and I pleaded my innocence that I was not complicit in any crime as far as I was concerned. There was never an intention to steal the marbles. It was the crack in the window that put paid to any defence. To this day I remember my cousin making his way to our house. I can still vividly recall him walking up to our door step with his leather jacket, huge flares, platform shoes and a distinctive moustache. You would think he was going to a disco rather than coming to complain, knowing full well I would receive the full wrath of my dad. He explained the situation to my dad in front of me. Not sure what to do, I stood still listening and thinking we did not take anything, it was just innocent kids having fun. We genuinely meant no harm. For my dad, who is a strict disciplinarian, he could not have any complaints about his kids. He was the authority and no kid of his would tarnish the family name. Well, there is always one. On this occasion he beat the shit out of me, so much that I pissed myself on the kitchen floor. My mum was stood there watching helplessly and my older brother was in the distance probably thinking thank fuck that wasn't me. In those days Esther Rantzen would have had a field day. Back in the 70s if you did wrong you would get a back hander and no one would bat an eyelid. It's also fair to say there was much more respect for authority and elders. Every generation hears the same story but it really was different.

Forward twenty or so years and both kids have taken different routes in life. It does make me think how fate, parents and your social circles can, to a point, dictate the outcome of your early life. Once you have taken a certain path it is extremely difficult to move away. As I have always maintained, kids are not born racist or delinquents, but the life around them can play them the wrong cards. It's like a game of poker for certain kids born into difficult families and surroundings.

If I had a real passion it was football. If my mum wanted to find me I would be playing football with friends or kids from the area. I would play day and night in the back garden or on the street. Anywhere we could find space, out would come the jumpers for posts. The youngest or the less mobile would go in goal and then we would play Wembley for hours. Street football could be rough playing with kids much older than you. They would not think twice about giving you a kick and after a while, you just think that's part and parcel of football. Even after school the first thing I would do after getting changed would be to practice my skills in the back garden. It was a small garden and I had to be extremely careful not to hit any windows. Without thinking, this actually increased my skill level as one hit on the window meant a backhander from my dad. Football was my life and all I wanted to do was to one day play for Coventry City Football Club.

SENT TO COVENTRY

Where we lived was a mixture of private and council housing. Post-war Coventry had a policy of providing homes for workers and most of the housing was constructed very quickly to accommodate the new influx of migrants and workers. Coventry became a boom town during the 50s and 60s, which naturally attracted workers from all over the UK and the world. It must be stressed that due to a shortage of workers, the UK government invited immigrants over to Britain from the Commonwealth. The city became host to a number of nationalities including many from Ireland, Scotland, South Asia and Jamaica. On arrival most people tended to live where they are familiar with people of their own nationality for safety and cultural reasons. They also tended to settle in the less desirable areas, which most of the time was all that was affordable. My dad explained that when he first arrived in Coventry during the mid 50s how he shared a two bedroom terraced house on Red Lane with 8 other people. They were here to initially work and earn enough money to give them an opportunity to make something of their lives back in India.

These men worked hard, as did most of the indigenous population – welfare was frowned upon and only existed for the really desperate or those incapable of working. Employment was such that you could leave one company in the morning and become employed elsewhere almost immediately. However, those from South Asia were limited to the jobs they could pursue and accepted the jobs most of the population did not want.

The work ethic amongst the Asians in general is such that they will work all day and all night for a better life. This has been instilled in all first and second generation kids. You have to work hard and have aspirations to be seen as a success. It's a case of deferred gratification. Work hard for a better life later on. Life is not necessarily about overindulging in the moment and having very little for a rainy day later on in life. While I am noticing change with many of the kids from Asian backgrounds having much more than previous generations, much of this is also due to their parents acquiring through hard work grand sums of money and not wanting their kids to go through the same problems or difficulties as them.

Parents should refrain from having this guilt factor and realise that these conditions made them what they are today. Whatever happens, though, it is very unlikely their children will end up living in desolation. It's merely making them understand and experience the value of life and money. If parents are not careful this can have repercussions and a detrimental effect on the kids growing up who have everything they need and not realise the value of a pound.

Through hard work and saving the first generation of Asians enabled themselves to purchase properties of their own while still sending money back to their respective families. In the 60s it was hard to even obtain a mortgage or a bank loan, thus so much respect needs to be given to people who managed to buy their own property.

At the back of Dunster Place was a grass verge area big enough to play football. I am still not sure of why the grass area existed, as it didn't really serve a purpose. However, we made use of the area by joining in with other kids to play five a side football. Well what started as five a side football would normally descend into a fight for all. I vividly remember playing one time and being nicknamed Sambo by one particular kid. He seemed to take pride in calling me Sambo every time I touched the ball. It was the norm and no one ever batted an eyelid. I always carried on as if that was the way life was. It didn't make it right but back in the late 70s that's just the way it was. What made this particular incident peculiar was that the kid was of mixed race and yet here he was calling me Sambo. I never did work that one out. Talking about names very few could pronounce my actual name correctly which was Sukhraj, so I was either known as Raj or George by many of the kids. In the end Raj was easy and has stuck with me ever since.

However, playing football was never easy. It was a free for all and no one ever knew who won as the scores could be so ridiculous. Kicking anyone and scrapping to win the ball was where I learned to defend myself and become an adroit player, nimble and fast off the mark. Most of the kids I played with were much older than me and at times I took a good kicking. Over time this is what helped me when I started to play for the school teams, as street football actually toughens you up and school football becomes an easier game.

Growing up in junior and senior schools I can honestly say I was either first or second to be chosen for the football team purely based on my pace. To be fair, I did possess some skill.

Racism was prevalent in the 70s and 80s and was part of growing up. I used to dread going to collect the Saturday Pink sports paper for my older brother. Each time I would go one particular lad in his late teens made it obvious he hated foreigners. He would throw stones and taunt with the same lyrics of Paki go home. It was almost weekly. I told my older brother, who didn't seem to take any notice. My mind started to open up about colour as this had never been an issue before, even at school. Our neighbours were good community people and looked after their own irrespective of colour.

One day I had had enough of being bullied on a Saturday afternoon. It became an ordeal and I dreaded 5.00pm as it was my duty to purchase the Pink sports paper. I was genuinely fearful that sooner or later he was going to beat the crap out of me. Eventually I told my neighbour, Mark Springer, who could look after himself. Opposite us lived Tony Birchall, another tough lad who hung out with the famous Coventry boxer Errol Christie. One Saturday after being harassed by this lad I met Mark on my way home. Distressed, I explained the situation to him and exaggerated a little. Mark got together with Tony and a few other lads and went looking for this illiterate idiot. All I remember is seeing Mark a few days later with his hand in a bandage. God only knows the damage to the other lad. Suffice to say I never saw that idiot again. That was our community; everyone stuck together.

BEHIND CLOSED DOORS

My early school memories are vague, though I do remember my first day and being sat next to a lad called Steven Powell. I thoroughly enjoyed my primary school days at Parkgate School, as it was like being on holiday. Unfortunately I was never an outstanding academic, though the endeavour to do well was always evident. They were really good days where I made some great friends.

I very nearly never made it to Parkgate Junior School. At the end of my primary years the Headteacher stated to my dad that the catchment area for where we lived was John Shelton School. Without putting up a fight, he duly enlisted me at John Shelton. I only lasted two days as I hated the school. It was grey and old and had a bad feel about the place. My dad took me back to see the Head Master of Parkgate, explaining that all my cousins and older brother had attended Parkgate and, more importantly, I had been in tears for days. They allowed me back in which was a godsend. It's amazing how even primary and junior schools can have an effect on kids psychologically, yet as adults we make these decisions for kids without understanding the impact.

Life at Parkgate Junior School was equally as enjoyable as primary school. It just had a fun element with some great teachers. I always believe a child's time at a school can have a positive or negative impact on their later lives. The teachers could never understand me. I was either delivering a high standard of work one day, or not interested the next. I have a very short attention span. I have learnt to focus and concentrate when required, but at school if I was bored it was time to switch off and start dreaming. Indolent comes to mind.

I used to enjoy assembly and sing my heart out to the hymns played each morning. I still feel assembly is an important part of any school and should continue to teach Christian values pertinent to the society we live in. The hymns or teachings did not make me any less of a Sikh; rather it taught me values and a universal language we could all adhere to.

Christianity was not forced upon us. To continue to learn about the Sikh religion I could go to the temple during the week or weekends. I know of a number of kids of all different faiths that enjoyed the morning assembly – bring it back, it serves a purpose.

While I thought of myself as a tough kid I rarely got into fights. I had to act tough due to where I was from and being quite tall for my age at the time certainly helped. In all honesty fighting was not my thing and never has been, although growing up in a patriarchal Sikh family can be hard at the best of times. Sikhs by nature are known as warriors due to their history. Living in a family of all boys made life even tougher. My dad would feel ashamed if someone complained about me and certainly knew how to strike fear in me. Yet my mum was the compassionate one, and someone who you would go to for comfort, yet she also demonstrated an amazing mental strength. She never shouted at us and always wanted the best for us. My older brother Jas had the burden of responsibility and the only one who got away with it all was my younger brother Sonny. I am not saying all Sikh families are similar. However, most do play up to the stereotypical Sikh of not walking away from a confrontation. Sikhs can be a riotous lot and that's just the women! They will shoot you first and ask questions later. With almost all Sikhs descending from a farming background, many land arguments in Punjab are known to be settled with killings and murders. That's just with the brothers and sisters. In all seriousness, the paradox is that Sikhs are probably one of the most generous and tolerant people in the world. They are an open and caring community. If you go to a Sikh house you will not leave without eating and drinking enough for days and the hospitality is more than generous. If you need assistance the Sikhs are always there to help. It's no wonder the Sikhs are celebrated for their fearless fighting in the two great World Wars and are a respected nation throughout the world. In Britain, with many of the third generation Sikh kids growing up in a western society, the issue of confrontation and acting riotously is slowly disappearing. We are becoming much calmer I think!

As a family during the 1970s we enjoyed holidays, though not in the modern sense. Our holidays did not consist of travelling to Spain, France or exotic shores further afield. Our holidays were much closer to home. They were spent in one of the great towns of the Black Country – Wolverhampton or Bulberhampton as many of my parent's generation would pronounce! I had no concept of holidays abroad and would count Wolverhampton as one of our regular destinations. The reason for this was due to my mum's side of the family living here.

For several years we would either travel to Wolverhampton during our school holidays or our relatives would make the short trip to Coventry. I absolutely enjoyed my time in Wolves as my two cousins, Bob and Nindy, were similarly aged and just as adventurous as me. They lived in Prosser Street, which was an area where many immigrants from South Asia and Jamaica had decided to settle in the 50s and 60s. I remember the train lines behind the rows of terraced housing where we would play all the time. The pub on the corner of the street had a shutter where you could purchase crisps and soft drinks without having to venture inside. This was new to me as I had never seen such a pub in Coventry. Although I loved visiting my cousins, it was great coming back to Coventry, which appeared at the time to be modern and clean.

At school I remember the beginning of term when all the kids would discuss their summer holidays. Some had just returned from Spain, some from Greece, some had even stayed in England at the new family holiday parks. When it came to my turn I just simply said I went to Wolverhampton for two weeks. I can vividly remember the look on those kids' faces, racking their brains trying to figure out in which part of the world Wolverhampton could be found. When I explained it was in the Black Country, they all smiled believing I had gone to the Caribbean or somewhere similar. I had a permanent tan so I guess I got away with it for a few years. For a short while I was quite popular as many would ask me questions about my exotic holiday. No palm trees but plenty of yam yams!

It's also important to play or participate in sports, as this is where you really learn to become a leader and a team player. I absolutely loved football and played day and night. At the time my favourite players were the Coventry City legends Ian Wallace, Garry Thompson and Mick Ferguson, who unbeknown to me at the time were to become good friends later on in my life.

1978 was a special year as it was the year my older brother got married. He was six foot, broad and a smart looking guy. It was also his influence that introduced me to different genres of music and of course football. A friend of my dad's knew of a family in Birmingham looking for a suitable groom for their daughter. After the initial introductions both families were happy to proceed and this was an exciting time for all concerned. My dad spared no expense to ensure he gave my brother the best wedding he could afford. The wedding itself took place at a school hall in Birmingham. Asian weddings are full of colour, ceremonies, drink and food. It really is an exciting spectacle and every generation has its time.

The couple were happy for several months. However, what transpired over the next year or so left a lasting psychological effect on the whole family.

As was custom and in many cases still is, the bride returns to the groom's house and they live together with the extended family until they have saved enough for a house. This was normal and nothing out of the ordinary. Unfortunately some families also have a disposition not to see others do so well and, in our case, certain outside influences conspired to make the marriage a failure, which brought no end of tears and misery to my immediate family. Over time the constraints started to show and began affecting my brother and his wife. Being so young I did not see her as a sister-in-law, she was more like my sister. It was great to speak to someone without the bravado; she was similar to my mum in that she was compassionate. She was born in England and so could communicate with us on that level.

One particular incident was the point of no return in their already strained marriage. We were invited to a wedding party. On this occasion both our families and my sister-in-law's immediate family were attending. My dad was unable to attend due to work commitments. In this party, and as has been custom until a few years ago, women sat separately from the men. It was at the Jubilee Crescent Community Centre in Radford, Coventry. Towards the end of the evening the family friend who had arranged the marriage came into the women's room and began making threatening statements to my mum in earshot of everyone. The words were offensive enough to make my mum emotional and feel ashamed in the presence of her peers. You need to remember my mum is not one for confrontation and all her life she has given to people and never thought ill of anyone. She is an absolute pious character who respects all human beings irrespective of their race, religion, creed or colour. For me any man who can belittle a female of her character in front of others is nothing but a coward. My mum left the party immediately. Rushing back home my dad's sister came back with us to comfort my mum. My dad, on receiving a call from my brother, rushed back from his place of work. When he discovered the true facts and that his close friend had betrayed him he completely lost it. He was so full of anger he picked up the ceremonial sword most Sikhs stored in their house in those days and, with my older brother, went looking for this particular person with my auntie in tow to stop him. This was turning into a nightmare. He was so angry I am convinced to this day that he would have killed him. It wasn't just the betrayal but his friend had committed one of the biggest cardinal sins in insulting another man's wife. I had never seen him like this before. This was pure rage; you could see the anger in his eyes.

As a ten-year-old you are sat at home helpless and try to make sense of the situation. I was powerless to do anything. I didn't even know how to comfort my mum as, growing up in a male dominated family, I never really got to understand the meaning of compassion or have the ability to show emotion. I did not know what the concept really meant. Perhaps if I had a sister life may have been different and I would be much more conversant with being able to express my feelings. Fortunately the wedding party had finished and everyone had left the Community Centre. On returning home my dad was still livid, though my auntie had managed to calm him down. He just felt so let down by this whole episode. This was just the warm up as things were about to heat up later that evening.

One of our relatives decided it was a good idea to bring my sister-in law's father to our house later that evening. He was drunk, aggressive and did not need much encouragement to start an argument. It was only a matter of time before sparks would fly. On arrival, there were several accusations about our family of mistreating his daughter, which was completely untrue and quite the contrary. My father stayed calm, knowing a wrong move could jeopardise the relationship. This man was not leaving and became more and more threatening. At this point my mum called her brother from Wolverhampton and he arrived within half an hour with his sons. One of his sons, a former soldier who had served with the Singapore forces, was ready for anything. He was 6ft tall, broad and could look after himself. He was also very close with my dad. At one particular moment my brother's father-in-law, who was also 6ft and broadly built, challenged my father to a fight. Without thinking, my dad got up and told him to take a swing if he had the guts. All hell was about to break loose. At the same time my uncle's sons got up and asked the accuser to take a step outside to finish this off. Let's just say the father-in-law saw sense, sobered up and sat back down, realising he was about to get pounded.

After a while things calmed down and my brother's father-in-law was persuaded to leave. As far as we were all concerned he was on his way back to Birmingham. A crazy episode over; well, that's what we thought. The guys in the house, and there were a few, decided to go to the pub and made their way to The Bantam pub on Hen Lane. After half an hour the father-in law appeared again out of nowhere. Banging on our door, he was let in by his daughter, hoping he would calm down. What I witnessed next had a major impact on me psychologically. He went to the kitchen looking for a knife and threatened to kill my mum. My auntie, terrified, asked me to accompany her to the pub to get my father and uncles. All the way to the Bantam I was scared for my mum, with tears rolling down my cheeks, not knowing if my mum was going to be fine.

When we got to the Bantam I ran in and said the knob had returned and was causing trouble. In no time the men arrived back home, this time ready to give this guy the beating of his life. He had made a run for it and was gone before my dad and the others arrived. You could feel the tension in the house. Not sure of the facts at this stage as I was upstairs hiding. That night I remember vividly standing in front of the Lord's picture vowing for revenge when I was older. I was confused, angry and extremely scared.

That night left an indelible mark on my life and I can still remember every little detail. The psychological impact this had on me only came to light years later. I became scared of sleeping in the dark and would awake at the slightest of noises. My mum became concerned as I started to sleep talk at night and would sometimes wake up in the middle of the night sweating. My bravado disappeared. I became an introvert and stopped playing out as much as I used to. Such effects on kids can leave a lasting impression and have an impact on their adult life. It took a while before I began to regain my confidence. Just walking from school after football practice during the winter months was an ordeal. I would literally run back home. Even going to Coventry town centre on a Saturday afternoon was an ordeal. It was a difficult, depressing couple of years for me personally. I bottled everything up and this made matters worse. I had absolutely no idea or concept of how to release my emotions – there was no outlet.

In reality I just learned to deal with the situation and on the whole I have been fortunate to have had a happy-go-lucky life with a few blips in between for good measure. However, after all the personal issues I had to contend with, I have learned to forgive and move on. The simple act of forgiveness frees your mind and removes all the negative obstacles that can potentially prevent you from progressing. It allows you to channel all your positive energy, spirit and resource to achieve what you want. Harbouring negative images or thoughts will only cause harm to you. I do not know of any family who has not had to contend with some sort of problem and, in many ways, this part of adulthood helps you to cope with whatever life throws at you.

Even during my darkest moments I would find solace in the Lord and believed the good times were around the corner. This mindset of constantly visualising a positive outcome became a coping mechanism. It also became a component that I learned to take advantage of when I needed a positive uplift. I had dreams and huge ambitions and this is the reason why I continued to push and challenge myself. Since I can remember, I have always had an inherently positive outlook on life and have the natural ability to be self-motivated. I am amazed that schools do not provide teachers with support to assist kids to think positively. There will always be some sort of problem in anyone's life; it's something we will never move away from. However, teaching kids from early on how they can maintain a positive mental attitude can go a long way to alleviating a sense of failure or coping with personal issues.

TICKET TO INDIA

My story of understanding achievement began when I was 14 and doing my CSEs and 'O' levels at President Kennedy School in Coventry. Not a recognised academic or high-flyer, I was one of those students who just went through the system without any fuss. I was a teacher's dream – never failing to turn up to school, handed my homework in on time and never gave anyone any trouble. At the end of five years I collected my results and achieved 2 'O' levels English (grade B) and Sociology (grade B). My parents as you can imagine coming from an Asian background were distraught. What was their son going to do now – the hopes of becoming a doctor, accountant and dentist were well and truly dashed!

President Kennedy Comprehensive School was a mere twenty minute walk from my house. Most, if not all, the local kids walked to school. Very few came by car and those who lived a distance travelled by bus. The school is situated on Rookery Lane and is one of the larger secondary schools in Coventry, with approximately 1,500 students. The first year literally came and went due to the teachers' strike. I remember the strike was during the first term in 1981, when the snow never seemed to disappear. There would be snow fights to and from school. We had weekly homework set which would be completed on the same day. The rest of the week I would be out playing football with my mates. When we finally returned to school our registration was in huts which were absolutely freezing. They were so poorly assembled that students would break into them each night and cause all sorts of chaos.

The second year was a little vague and I can hardly remember the year. What I can recall, however, is the five blocks at the school. Each year you would progress to the next until you finally hit Block 5. By the time I got there it needed a complete revamp. The school was developed in the 60s with a music block surrounded by a pond, which was a pretty feature. Pretty until the older kids decided to throw you in the pond for their amusement. It was also during the second year that my family travelled to India to give me my first trip abroad. In fact it was my first trip on an aeroplane. My grandfather had become very ill so my mum, who had not returned to India since she first became married, wanted to see him before he passed away. The school gave me special dispensation to go and I had four weeks off school in February 1983. In order to compensate the school set me some homework. Stupidly I took the homework and extra work with me. There I was carrying two solid bags full of school work. I should have known better as I never once looked at my books and the teachers never questioned me.

We travelled by Japan Airlines, as my uncle secured the tickets for a good price as he was an agent in Southall. I wasn't sure if it was do with his commission but he secured the tickets nevertheless. Leaving from Heathrow I clearly remember the massive airport and hundreds of people. It was like something out of a film. The plane itself was huge and it was all very exciting. The plane stopped off to refuel at Abu Dhabi and I remember these people of Indian heritage getting on with these enormous music systems and other electrical equipment. I'm not sure this would be allowed in today's climate.

On arrival, I can still remember the heat hitting us as we departed from the plane. Delhi airport seemed fine though, and I was just excited to be visiting another country. While I had heard several stories about India and, in particular, Punjab, I had no real concept of what life would be like. Customs was easy enough and to greet us all were my grandfather and uncle. Our first stop was my uncle's house in Delhi. The bungalow was beautiful and set in huge grounds. I wasn't sure what his profession was but I guessed he had a good job. We stayed here for a couple of days and to be honest I thought India was brilliant after my initial experience.

On the third day we made our way to Delhi train station for our long trip to the Punjab. My father bought first-class tickets and I was feeling like a king. On taking our seats I quietly mentioned to my dad that we had sat in the wrong carriage. This was definitely economy class. Staring straight back at me my dad made it clear this was first-class. I protested, claiming he was wrong. The seats were worn out, there was no carpet and some kid kept walking up and down the aisle selling magazines, drinks, crisps, in fact you name it he could get it. After much protestation I realised this really was first-class and to make matters worse I was about to endure a 10 hour train ride. Welcome to India!

After travelling for what seemed like an eternity we finally arrived in Ludhiana, Punjab. On departing the train a porter took our bags. How he could carry so many bags with every part of his anatomy still shocks me to this day. These guys are so strong it amazes me. Yet they never complain and work hard all day for a pittance. It's times like these when you realise how lucky we really are in the Western world. Someone will always pick you up in the UK. In countries like India they will not touch you in fear of being questioned for murder or assault. The station at Ludhiana was absolutely packed and, as my grandfather was accustomed to the town, he led us out to the taxi rank. Here we had another journey to the village of Sidhma, which was in the district of Nakodar.

The journey to our village was a half-hour ride. What struck me immediately was the number of beggars and a child with no limbs travelling on a skateboard type of vehicle to get around. Now don't get me wrong, I was 12 at the time and aware of the situation in India but nothing really captures the reality of life until you see it first hand. The roads were bumpy with pot holes Glasgow would be proud of. Dirt was everywhere and there was a distinct smell in the air. Nothing unpleasant, just a smell I will always associate with India.

On arriving at our village, I remember half the population waiting to greet us. One by one all these uncles, aunties, and kids met us. I was overwhelmed. I had never experienced anything like this before. Then suddenly a young girl appeared and took my suitcase off me and at the same time explained she was my sister. I thought nothing of it until she said she was my real sister. Next came another woman who claimed to be my mother and then said she really was my stepmother. This I realised was my father's divorced wife, who had remained in the family home due to my grandfather refusing to let her go back to her parents' village. There were so many relatives I was becoming confused.

Once inside the brick walled house, or a building that resembled a house but looked nothing like one, I was greeted by a number of people squashed inside. This really was the mother of all greetings. One by one they introduced themselves, which in itself became exhausting. So far I had met my non-biological sister, so-called mum and suddenly there was a young lad sat near me who was now introduced as my brother. This was too much to take; I genuinely believed these were all my real brothers and sisters. I looked at my dad, thinking you've been busy? As is the custom, they were merely friends and relatives who for affection in the Asian culture use the word brother or sister.

After an hour of introductions and staring at the brick walled house both my brother and I broke into floods of tears. This was not what I imagined of India. We were in hell and for four weeks. My brother and I wanted to go back home to Coventry. To make matters worse I needed to go for a pee and was told the toilets were outside. After looking around I came back in to say I could not find the outside toilet. Everyone started laughing, which got me thinking was it so obvious that I missed the toilet? In fact there were no toilets. I had to go to the field for a pee and a number two. I could live with pissing in the street but the number 2 was going to prove tricky.

When you have no choice in a situation you do what it takes and let's just say I adapted to the environment. Not a great example but this principle applies to life in general. We all come across difficult situations which we need to assess and adapt to. For me India, and especially Punjab, was going to be a journey where I really needed to adapt and quickly. Fortunately for me, my dad being a man of certain standards, where everything needs to be clean and in order, my grandfather's house did not appeal to him.

The fundamental reason for visiting India was to meet my mother's father, who was severely ill and wished to see his daughter before he passed away. The timing could not have been worse; he died literally days before we arrived at the village. On arriving at my Grandfather's village a very different greeting awaited us. On this occasion the mood was completely sombre; we knew we had arrived too late. My mum, as expected, was extremely emotional as she had not seen her father for almost 15 years. Fate plays many games with people's lives and it's only when we lose loved ones that for a few moments we attempt to become philosophical and put life into perspective. Life should be simple, yet we complicate matters with the worldly pressures of pleasing people. Even to this day, when I hear people introduce friends or family or people they know of, I can pretty much guarantee the introduction ends with what profession or how affluent that person is. It's as if we live in a society which looks down on people who may not have the prototype professional position or drive about in a brand new

Range Rover. To be financially secure is absolutely fine and money gives you choices, but the point I am making is how we make those choices and who we decide to socialise with. Normal, hard-working people are also humans and less conniving than many of the so-called richer types I can think of.

After meeting our cousins we were taken in to my grandfather's accommodation, which was almost a replica of my dad's house. I was more comfortable here as my cousins were of similar age. After a few hours the younger one, who was about 15, took me for a wander around the village. It was great to get out and, as I spoke fluent Punjabi, we got on really well. That was until he started to hold my hand and every so often kiss me on the cheek. I did not take kindly to such affection. Every time he held my hand I immediately moved it away. I made it clear I was uncomfortable and there was no way I was turning for anyone, especially in a Punjabi village. He was totally bemused. He genuinely did not believe he was doing anything wrong or out of the ordinary. Apparently men in India view holding hands in public as normal and it is simply a cultural aspect of that society. Culture or not I was having none of it.

After paying our respects and meeting our cousins we decided after a few days to move on to my auntie's place a few miles away. There she had two young teenage sons who I could hang out with and we enjoyed a much better standard of living, but still no toilet. Adapt we did. One morning I decided to have a shower and could not find one. Surely they had a cleaning area, even if I had to use a bucket. For me the cleaning facility was out in the yard in a kind of well with cold water flowing. I was in and out in quick time, every time. There were a number of properties situated close to my auntie's in a type of cul de sac where other families lived. My auntie was comfortable and had a steady income via the land she inherited from her husband. Tragically, her husband was murdered in Calcutta where he worked while the kids were young. My dad and his brother paid for the wedding and sent money over for a number of years, which was expected and the norm at the time.

Many people who came over from India to work in the UK came primarily to earn enough money to give their families back in India a chance to improve their lifestyle. Over time the idea was to return back to India. As we all know this never materialised and the UK became their new adopted home. However, she had two servants. There was one young lad known as Paresh and an older guy, both from Eastern India. They only spoke Hindi and broken English. It is amazing how language is universal, as we communicated with each other very well. During the days I would spend time with them while they were working away in the fields or tending to the animals. I was intrigued by them. Their families were thousands of miles away and they were living in a shack. My auntie looked after Paresh's wages and would give him the money every six months for him to send back to his family. For Paresh this was an excellent arrangement, as his food and lodgings were paid for. I became good friends with Paresh and tried to understand his background and his aspirations. Although only a teenager he was working over 12 hour shifts. His dream was to eventually own a piece of land for him and his family. Part of his wages was to provide the upkeep of his mother, father and brothers and sisters. The other half was to save for a new life. I may only have been twelve but I understood what dreaming and aspirations were about. Paresh had ambition, yet most people would not talk to him with any respect and just treated him like a second class citizen. To me he was another human being and one who taught me so much about life and pursuing your ambitions. To be fair to my auntie, and especially my mum and dad, Paresh was treated like family.

While in India one of my so-called sisters was getting married so we experienced a new meaning to weddings. In India everyone attends, there is enough food to feed a village and the dancing goes on all night. As you can imagine, even back in the early eighties, it was show time. The groom's family turned up with a handful of guys carrying rifles, which I actually found fascinating. As the drinks began flowing they suddenly became trigger happy until one of them shot a local in the backside by mistake. All hell broke loose as people started shouting and blaming one another. The poor victim was lying on the floor in absolute agony. I had never seen anyone shot, never mind seen a real gun before. This was like the American western film OK Corral, except this was not OK in Punjab. Tensions quickly dissipated as the elderly leaders took control and transported the poor man to hospital. The wedding continued without any further issues. Suffice to say the poor man lived to see another day. He certainly took one for the team. I have been to several weddings over the years, all glamorous, with each wedding outshining the previous. At a recently attended wedding a helicopter was booked to fly the bride and groom to the afternoon party; but nothing will ever beat this poor man being shot up the arse! The trip to India was enjoyable, though I was starting to get bored. After four weeks I was pleased to be back home and able to use simple facilities we take for granted such as the toilet or hot water when showering with the famous Indian bucket!

While out in India my auntie introduced us to a local family friend of hers who had an educated daughter looking to get married. With my brother's divorce finalised my auntie saw this as an opportunity to start the brokering. My mum and dad were not really enthusiastic, as they were still coming to terms with the aftermath of the divorce. However my auntie insisted. In all honesty they just wanted their daughter to get to England as do most people in India. This was her ticket to the promised land. My brother did marry her a few months later and I felt for him, as he had never really recovered from his first marriage. Whether he was trying to please my parents I cannot say for certain, as we have never spoke of the subject, but the marriage was over as soon as it began. It was doomed from the beginning as the two were worlds apart.

Our family was in a dreadful state; we were lost souls who just did not know which way to turn. Such issues can have a psychological and detrimental effect on any young person. It affects your personality and social skills. The repercussion for our family was something out of hell. If the first break up was bad this was worse. My dad and brother had to endure threats and other unsavoury accusations. We were completely shunned from some close friends and families. Although I was young at the time, you do have an understanding and try to make sense of the situation. The first divorce knocked my confidence and bravado. This time I was becoming an angry child; inside I was hurting. I needed a way out. I could not speak to anyone for fear of being misunderstood. This probably explained why I only wanted to be around select friends. I was looking for comfort; to get away from the hell I was experiencing at home. I began mixing with the wrong people at school, which affected my studies. The only place I could find an outlet was on the football park or listening to music. It was a form of escapism. For several hours I would forget about the real world and issues I did not want to face. Any child's formative years are so critical and I do understand when kids react at school or rebel. Most of this is to do with their home lives. I found solace in some great friends who probably didn't realise they were providing me with an outlet to get away from the issues affecting me mentally.

One of my close friends at the time who I must thank is Pommy Dhadda, a lad I grew up with throughout my school years from Parkgate to President Kennedy. Our friendship kept me sane. Eventually we went our separate ways.

Reflecting back on my childhood years, I know a great deal of my personality is shaped by my experiences good and bad. However, those dark days from the ages of 9 to 13 left a lasting impression on me and I still think about those times to this day, though I have learned to leave the past and not let those issues affect my future. Forgiveness is essential to move on and it frees your mind to focus on the important things in life.

As a family we developed a siege mentality. We became closer, as if there was a proverbial ring around us no outsider could penetrate. From that moment onwards we became fiercely loyal to one another. The trait has remained with me to this day. It's something I have instilled in my kids. Your immediate family are the only ones who care and will look out for you when most others would turn away. It's my positive can do attitude that keeps me from the negativity that we are surrounded with. The inner determination and motivation to succeed during the most difficult times is something I cannot explain, but became part of me during my most challenging period. Even when most of our families and friends turned the other cheek, I would be sat alone in my bedroom in profound thought, thinking of the good times ahead and visualising a better future. There was certainly someone in the ether looking after us.

SKINHEADS, RIOTS, ANTI-NAZI LEAGUE – WELCOME TO THE 80S

From 1980 to the summer of 1983 I felt a dark cloud constantly hanging in the air. Life was gritty, cold and dark. Unemployment was rising and communities were faced with hardship. Many areas of the UK experienced a breakdown of social cohesion. Disorder and riots began to dominate the evening news. Nationalism was on the rise. The society I knew had suddenly become a living nightmare. There was uncertainty in almost all types of industry. Overnight I witnessed a cultural change with the emergence of skinheads. At first this was a fashion statement and I am proud to say I had a skinhead and my very own pair of brown Doc Martens. I was proud to be a young skinhead. My dad was absolutely fine with it, though I did pester him for the boots. Initially I wanted the Black Doc Martens but the local shoe shop, known as Tudor Bar, kept a limited stock of all shoes. Unfortunately the black boots had sold out. I desperately wanted the Doc Marten boots so accepted the brown colour. I had the whole gear, a Harrington jacket, skin tight jeans and my Docs.

The Specials, The Selector, The Jam and The Clash were bands I enjoyed listening to. The music was full of energy and different to what we had previously experienced. We wanted to be part of something different, a movement challenging the status quo. The music had an exciting edge to it. Politics and music were inseparable. The disco scene was still there dominating the music charts alongside the explosion of new social politically conscious bands. I was also witnessing a cultural shift associated with the music. Bands such as the Specials and the Clash gave kids a voice. While there were mods and rockers a new subculture was emerging once again.

Suddenly the skinhead movement appeared overnight. The skinhead culture originally came from Jamaica and was influential during the 60s. It was black and white kids enjoying ska music. Skinheads during the late 70s and early 80s became synonymous with the far right. The atmosphere in Coventry turned for the worse. Asians were targeted and used as scapegoats for the rising unemployment. At local places of worship we were told not to visit the town centre as it was becoming increasingly dangerous for Asians. For whatever reason, it felt as though Coventry had become the hub for the far right. It wasn't just Coventry, it felt the UK was in a state of chaos and disarray. There were pitched battles between the National Front and the Anti-Nazi League. Communities and the youth were fighting against a backdrop of injustice, discrimination and police brutality. Britain was on fire and would leave an epoch that still reverberates to this day.

During the summer of 1981 I remember attending an anti-fascist march with my dad and younger brother Sonny. This was as much to do with the racist murder of Satnam Gill earlier in Coventry as it was to do with the increase in racist attacks. People had had enough of being targeted and abused and were ready to make a stand. The constant worry of going out and being attacked or abused was getting too much to take. There was a lack of confidence and trust in the police and it had got to the point where many of the immigrants had no choice but to stand up and be counted alongside the indigenous people of our country. There was only so much abuse people could tolerate. Anger was reaching boiling point and many older Asian kids began standing up to the fascists. Something had to give. Being 11 years of age at the time, the march for me was more like a carnival at first. There were so many people, black and white, in unison laughing and talking to one another. This was a civil rights march and it felt like the whole of Coventry had turned out to protest against the ongoing racial problems. The day was not going to pass peacefully as the National Front had organised a counter protest the same day.

The anti-racist march started from Foleshill Road, an area where many of the immigrants had first moved to. The first incident occurred before the march had even set off. A bus travelling towards Bedworth, a small village north of Coventry, almost had its windows completely smashed. On the top deck a handful of far right activists decided it would be an intelligent idea to fly the NF flag. What they failed to realise was the bus had to make a stop to pick up passengers in the middle of Foleshill, where the march was to start from. Fortunately for those youths, the bus driver refused to open the doors, as anti-racists surrounded the bus and were baying for blood. That really set the scene. All was well until we reached the centre of town near the cathedral. The atmosphere was tense. You just knew one incident could spark a riot. There were a line of police separating the fascists and the anti-Nazi league. Then suddenly all hell broke loose. You could hear police sirens everywhere, helicopters hovered above and the whole place descended into chaos. People began running everywhere; it was becoming quite frightening. Admittedly I was scared, regretting ever coming along. Youths black, white and Asian were running all over place. This was a full scale riot. Toxteth, Handsworth, Southall, St Paul's, Brixton and now Coventry made the headlines on the evening news. The police struggled to contain the protestors. My dad remained calm and walked us through the subway at Pool Meadow to the local Gurudwara, where my older brother eventually picked us up. That day I decided any future protests would be best channelled from home; this really was not my scene. I remember several years later sitting in the Pilot pub in Coventry discussing the anti-fascist march with boxing legend Errol Christie. He claimed to have beaten up more right wing skinheads in an hour during the riots than at any other time in his life. I decided against explaining I made a hasty retreat and was probably sat at home watching Love Thy Neighbour!

Another incident I remember was in 1981 as a first year leaving President Kennedy School to go home. Unfortunately I was the first to leave after the school bell had rung and, while waiting for my brother to pick me up in his car, an older lad headed for my direction. I guessed something was not right as I noticed his fist was clenched. Out of nowhere he started punching me in the face. With blood everywhere and on instinct I ran into the road. Luckily there were no cars about, otherwise this could have been serious. The lad simply walked back to the shop where all the kids hung out as if nothing had happened. It was a random cowardly attack. When my brother arrived I explained the situation and he went looking for the coward with me in tow and blood and tears running down my face. He could not find the culprit. Rest assured, I was never the first to leave the school gates. Looking back we never reported the incident to the school or the police and just got on with life. Can you imagine such an incident today? There would be an outcry and rightly so. Back in the early eighties if you had the shit kicked out of you it was just a case of bad luck.

On another occasion an older Asian lad was attacked by a fellow pupil and when he reacted and actually gave the other kid a hiding, he had to be protected by the authorities. There were skinheads outside the school gates waiting for this Asian lad and the teachers had no power once we were outside the school. The police had to be called in and drove him home for several weeks until the situation calmed down. This did not even make the local papers. This was life; everyone just gone on with it. I know many Asian kids at President Kennedy School professed to being close friends with boxer Errol Christie, even though they had never met him, just to stay safe. Looking back, nothing ever really happened but you still needed your wits about you.

School was becoming unpredictable at this particular time. Asians were not really known for fighting or to get involved in trouble due to having to face the wrath of their fathers later. It was bad enough being chased by thugs, but to then have the police at the door because your son was caught fighting was not something any Asian parent could accept or tolerate. The police were generally not trusted and had a reputation for being discriminatory. The last thing a parent wanted was to draw attention from the police.

It must be stressed that not all skinheads were politically motivated and many did protect some of the vulnerable kids. I am not sure most young adults going out Paki bashing had any idea of politics. These were the same people who would think nothing of having a curry at their favourite Indian restaurant at the weekend. This was life and we just got on with it. In many ways the victims appeared to tolerate racism as part of general life. With little or no police protection you had to fend for yourself, and some Asian lads I know began to fight back at school.

School life can reinforce views of the outside world. Once we played Foxford Comprehensive School in a football match. Charanjit and I were the only Asians in the Kennedy team while the Foxford line up was 90% Asian. I didn't really think anything of it, as it was a game of football for me. At half-time one of my team mates started to complain to our P.E. teacher that the

Foxford team comprised of too many Pakis. The teacher, who was a respected member of staff, just smiled and never once reprimanded the kid. He actually made a joke of the situation, which in my mind sent a message to say its fine to talk of certain cultures in a derogatory manner. If the teacher who is regarded as an upstanding person of society and there to teach right from wrong thought nothing of it, as kids you begin accepting a situation as acceptable and the norm. The incredulous point here was Charanjit and I were not even taunted or subjected to any racism from our own team. This brings me back to familiarity. We were friends with most of our team players and they saw us as one of them. They appeared to look beyond colour and religion once they got to know us. The year was 1983 not 1963.The purpose of each day was to either avoid the issue or not let it bother you. I had a mixture of friends and being a decent footballer I believe for this reason protected me from any incidents among my peers. There were kids in my year who would think nothing of explicitly name calling or bullying Asian kids. Playing football with them got me off the hook. They looked upon me as one of them. It also makes you think as to whether these kids really were racist or prejudiced; did they understand politics or was it because they saw some kids as different and that was the excuse to bully or target someone? Or was it because they were hearing and learning from their parents?

When society experiences unemployment and a breakdown in social cohesion, excuses and scapegoating becomes the trend. I had a good set of mixed friends and, because of where I was from, I always mixed with kids from all backgrounds. I didn't see colour or religion; for me, if they liked football, we became mates. I generally had a trouble-free life at school and I maintain much of this is to do with me being one of the lads when playing for the school football team. Having learnt street soccer I could hold my own and would never back out of a challenge. I may not have been a street fighter but I surely was a street footballer and one who was not too bad at it either. Football must be in the Athwal blood as my older brother had trials with Coventry Sporting and played several years in the Coventry suburban league for Dunlop while many of my cousins from Coventry played for the GNP team in the early 70s that went on to beat many of the top sides in the national football tournaments.

Even the music reflected the mood of the nation with the Specials number 1 single Ghost Town. It felt as if every city was under siege. Musically two-tone was at its height with bands such as the aforementioned the Specials, Selector, Madness and The Beat emerging. Life felt as if it was just one gritty conundrum.

It's unfair to present a negative image of the early 80s. Of course there were issues but we also enjoyed some great moments. The cliché that with every dark cloud is a silver lining is absolutely true. In moments of adversity and grief, if you try hard enough you can find times where you are in a proverbial dreamland. That one moment that gives you hope and faith for the future. They are the dreams to hold onto, grasp and not let go. It's during those difficult times that the positive images in your mind walks you through the minefields when all appears to be lost. We can all count on these experiences and beliefs. It's also about seizing those opportunities when they arise. It's not easy but you have to keep trying; after all life is a journey and will never be easy.

Being a dreamer, I could begin to visualise the future. Almost daily I would visualise a better world and place to live. This kept me motivated. The older you become, the more ideas you have for the future. The challenge then is to turn those ideas in to reality.

WIND OF CHANGE

For me the summer of 1983 was when I first noticed the wind of change. From 13 years of age I could feel my old self coming back to the fore. My confidence started to grow and I was becoming more attuned to enjoying life. I started to feel as if there was an air of optimism surrounding me. My life was about to begin a new chapter. The music scene was becoming mellow, with the new romantics taking over the air waves. Fashion became more affordable and the skinhead look disappeared overnight. Out went the tight trousers, Harrington jackets and cropped hair. The new wave consisted of large shoulderpad jackets, longer hair with blond highlights and brown streaks for the Asian kids, though some Asian lads I know experimented with blond dye and looked like freshies from India. The smart casual look became the fashion statement. Bands such as Spandau Ballet, Duran Duran, Wham, Frankie Goes to Hollywood and similar groups began to emerge. It was trendy to stand out. Something was happening to our society and it felt and looked good. The happiness I knew from years ago was back on the horizon. It's as if someone had turned the light back on and we had our blue skies back.

There were still anti-social issues with Asian kids but life was much more accepting. I had some really good school friends in Dean Flynn, Steven Dyal, Mark Cox, Michael McLoughlin and Bally Sonsoiy. It was my mates who showed me how to ride a moped. At the back of Dunster Place was a grass verge where we would occasionally find abandoned motorbikes. Once we discovered a scooter and, after a few hiccups, I was speeding up and down the verge. It was a stupid thing to do looking back but we were kids just having fun.

Life was on the up and I was enjoying the moment. During lunchtimes we would hang out at the top of the school fields near the train tracks. We would all just chill out in this place, which was peaceful and in many ways was our place.

In the third year you begin choosing the subjects you wish to study for your fourth and fifth years. There was now a purpose to school. I could choose what I wanted to do in the future. It was also the time when I was persuaded to attend our local temple, situated off Foleshill Road. In the past we only attended the Gurudwara on certain occasions. I was also shy of going to temples as there were so many people in the congregation, which made me feel uncomfortable. It was that feeling of everyone looking at you, even though in reality no one ever does. This probably goes back to my lack of confidence. However, for the first time in my life the Gurudwara which we started to attend showed me what peace of mind was all about. The congregation was small in number, which suited me and my confidence of being around so many people.

Enjoying the peace, I began attending each Sunday with my family. Ironically this also cost me my one passion – football. However, this is the time I became spiritually aware. I learned about humility, serving others and enjoying in the success of other people. While I always maintained my competitive edge, this was not compromised with envy or jealousy. For several years I lived a life that felt like utopia. There was no hatred or ill feeling to anyone. I was at ease with myself and enjoyed living. I concentrated on my plans and what I wanted to achieve in life. Such simplicity yet we make life so complicated. Or it begs the question, is life too complicated for us simple souls?

During the summer of 1983 I was hanging out with a good friend of mine, Dean Flynn. Walking past Holy Family school we noticed a training game on their football pitch. Dean knew one of the lads and called him over for a chat. Out of nowhere the coach appeared and asked if we wanted to attend the next training session. I was uncomfortable and mentioned to Dean that I would be the only Asian player training with the team. The fear of racism was at the forefront of my mind. The coach, on realising my concerns, made it clear everyone was welcome and I would have no issues. My first practice match was against the under 15s Holy Family team, an age group older than us. It was played at St Finnbars field and I just turned up with my boots. I played in my favourite position, right wing, due to my pace. The key incidents in the first half were me taking their left back apart and assisting one of our goals and then fouling one of their players. At this moment the racism came flooding back. It was a foul, though nothing serious, but the retaliation was vitriolic and back to the name calling of 'Paki this' and 'Paki that'. This was all in earshot of his manager and coach and yet not one of them reprimanded him. In today's society this would never be tolerated, but I just carried on as if it was part of life. To be fair to the player at the end of the game he apologised, but not after he kicked lumps out of me. Not deterred I continued to train with the under 14s and actually found this to be a decent squad. The next game was against the Under 13s and we completely annihilated them 10-1 with me scoring and assisting for a few of our goals. The manager was Mr Toal and his son David was in my year at Kennedy. The team was made up of Catholics, Protestants and two Sikhs, who were me and Steven Dyal. There was no religious intolerance and my team mates were absolutely superb with me. I was one of the lads. The irony here is that most of the players would end up fighting each other at the end of each school term. Cardinal Newman and President Kennedy were so close that regular fights would occur at the bottom of the Kennedy school gates on Watery Lane. At the time of joining Holy Family Football Club I was the only Asian in the team. However, I must stress that at no point was I subjected to any racism from my team mates. Race, religion and colour never came into the equation; I was simply one of the players. Sport clearly breaks down barriers and misconceptions people carry and for me the power of sport is one of the few mediums that had the power to bring communities together. After a few league matches I discovered I was being watched by Coventry scouts. My dad had other ideas and decided to pull the plug, as he felt it was interfering with my studies. The truth is he wanted me to attend the Gurudwara on Sundays. Mr Toal and his coach came around one Sunday to plead with my dad to let me continue playing and felt I had all the attributes to become a professional footballer. At that age it's so difficult to know how far your kids can develop, as you are never at your physical peak. In all honesty, at fourteen, I was good but not good enough, but it was great to know someone thought so. As previously mentioned my main strength was my pace; there were very few who could beat me over 100 metres. One lad who could and how he failed to become a professional footballer I will never know was Lee Nixon. We knew each other from Primary School and he is one footballer I knew who could win a match single-handed. To be fair we had several good players and would beat local schools at a canter. With Lee in the team at Parkgate Junior School we almost did the treble in 1981, winning the Coventry Schools Junior League and getting to two cup finals. We lost one memorable cup final 3-2 to Christ the King at Holbrooks School playing fields. The irony here was our Headmaster, Mr Bell, needed us to win as his wife was the Head at Christ the King. Either way the Kings couldn't lose.

President Kennedy was lucky to have some fantastic teachers at the time, one of whom was Miss Coe, who taught English and always kept faith in me. I was in the top set for English and, like my favourite team Coventry City, I would scrape through during term time exams to remain in the top set. English was my favourite subject at school but I would never really keep to the curriculum. I have lost count of the number of times I had to be reprimanded for writing essays on a completely different subject. The work would be to a really high standard. At the end of my fifth year Miss Coe mentioned that due to failing to provide the correct essays I should have been demoted to the second set, but felt that would have been an injustice due to the quality of work I was actually producing. Now that is great teaching as I finally emerged with a grade B in English.

Other great teachers of note included Mr Bonsor (English), Mr Foley (Sociology), Miss Merrell (Sociology), Mr White (History) and Mr Payne (History). I did notice an exodus of teachers during my upper sixth, many transferring over to Coundon Court School. As the saying goes nothing lasts forever. English and Sociology were my favourite subjects as demonstrated by my grades. The other subjects I simply chose because they were sciences and to be a doctor you had to choose sciences. Well, the doctor dream evaporated after the first term in the fourth year.

On the whole Kennedy was a good school and the teachers had been there for several years. The standard of education was good and, like any educational establishment, you get out what you put in to it. Not all kids are born to be doctors or scientists and should have the freedom to choose the subjects they can excel in and not be pressured by family and friends. In hindsight, I would have taken RE and music. Both these subjects at the time were open to ridicule from your peers. Yet RE for me would have been an easier 'O' level to pass and to play a musical instrument is a winner at any party.

During 1985/86, employment in the country started to improve. We began seeing the first glimpses of what the media termed yuppies. They had huge mobile phones, sharp suits, drank champagne and generally had a good time on extortionate salaries. I was in awe of these people. I wanted a piece of the action; I looked up to them. It's not money that's evil. Blame people not money. If used wisely money gives us choices and an opportunity to help one another. Wages were increasing and in general there was a good feel about life.

Again, music reflected society and Band Aid brought a whole generation of people together for a cause we initially were oblivious to. Clothes were an important fashion accessory. Being different and creative was important. Brands such as Lacoste, Fila, Ellesse and Tacchini became a social statement. People like me could only dream and window shop for such items, as they were too expensive for the average person. On one occasion I borrowed a pink Lacoste cardigan to wear to school. I felt like a million dollars, even if the rest of my clothes looked like a fashion disaster.

In the space of two years I had lost interest in playing competitive football and was more concerned about my education and contemplating University. This was also the year my older brother got married for a third time. I did personally struggle with all this marriage business. If the break-ups had a negative impact on me I would hate to think what my older brother must have gone through. After his third marriage I was adult enough to understand his situation, though remained cynical at the same time. It was not out of any disrespect to anyone; I just struggled with the situation. Perhaps I could never allow my first sister-in law to be replaced by anyone. She had such a positive effect on me that her leaving the family home was similar to losing a close family member. Such situations can leave an indelible mark on kids.

Over time I learned to deal with the situation and the old cliché time is a healer is absolutely true.

During my fifth year I made every conceivable attempt to time manage and pass as many exams as possible. The problem was I had no idea how to actually revise for an exam. All I was doing each evening was learning a topic parrot fashion. Obvious as it may seem, I had no understanding of the subject and just thought to write down as much as possible if the topic was even mentioned. Looking back, my revision was a waste of time and I could have used my time more productively doing something else. It's only at University that I gained a better understanding of revision and all by chance. I am one of those characters who will give everything for the cause, even if it's a loss leader. It's in the genes. I have a competitive streak and at times enjoy living on the edge when the odds are stacked against me. It's a trait that has been with me since my school days. Not always right, but not knowing when to give up has helped me more often than not. The summer months waiting for my results was agony. There is nothing worse when you walk out of exams than to start discussing the paper. Then you realise what you wrote down had nothing to do with the question. For me this problem appeared after every exam except for English and Sociology. I was clinging onto hope more than anything but knew deep down I would be lucky to gain a grade C in most of my subjects. I still kept the faith until the day arrived to collect my results.

I had arranged to meet my close pal Pommy and made my way to his house on Roland Avenue. We were both nervous though more hopeful than expectant; well I certainly was. On arrival, many of our friends had already arrived and knew their results. Happy faces everywhere – some got 6 passes, some seven though most passed with four. Surely I would get a minimum of four. My confidence was high after a few conversations; I had no doubt I would have a decent pass rate. In the hall I walked up to the teachers with a bit of a swagger, wearing my borrowed Lacoste jumper. The smile suddenly turned to horror. I had only passed 2 'O' Levels. The remainder were a combination of Ds and Es. Surely there was a mistake. The teachers looked at me as if to say try the YTS scheme, you may fare better. To make matters worse from a personal point of view, Pommy passed with over 4 'O' levels. For that second my world had come crashing down. There was obviously an element of envy and being one of the few who had not even achieved a minimum of four 'O' levels. What would I do next? How do I tell my parents? More importantly, what do they tell my relatives? To make matters worse, the calls began flooding in from friends and relatives whose sons and daughters had achieved five, six, even seven O' levels. Unfortunately, I just about mustered 2 – in my defence they were good grades though.

I spent the summer dwelling on what to do next. I even considered the YTS scheme. To add insult to injury, I even got turned down for an YTS office position. The government was content, as it meant they could fabricate the dole figures and leave all school leaving kids with a choice of either further education or a CPVE course, which was a complete farce and was for those students who had either failed their exams or had no idea of what to do next. I did attend one CPVE lesson after being persuaded by one of the teachers to do so and thought bollocks to this. The teachers, in my opinion, did not show any real concern for the welfare of students. You were really working your own way out in the big world. I personally did not have a one to one with any of the careers teachers. There were general discussions, though nothing more than what you already knew. I also felt there were low expectations of many of the students. Unless you were a student destined for University you were expected to leave school to pursue other avenues. The job of the school was complete when you hit 16!

After a couple of days in the sixth form, I somehow convinced an excellent teacher called Mr White to allow me to study History and Sociology 'A' Levels. This was unprecedented as you needed a minimum of 4 'O' levels to even think about 'A' Levels. The idea was for me to retake the 'O' Levels whilst studying for my 'A' Levels. Stroke of luck? Absolutely not. I made this happen as I believed in myself and persuaded the teachers to let me study 'A' Levels. This is the moment something happened. One day at home and thanking my lucky stars for a major break, I decided to write down what I wanted to achieve in my diary. My short term aspirations were to achieve the minimum number of 'O' levels and then to pass my 'A' levels to get me a place at University. At this point I had never read psychology books, though appeared to follow the mantra of believing that I would achieve a successful outcome. This was not me just saying it. I actually believed with all my heart that I would finally achieve what I wrote down in my diary.

Almost every day that passed I would remind myself of what I was going to achieve. Let's not get carried away, it was to just pass the exams at this stage. As time went on, I started to focus much more and genuinely believed that I would pass my exams.

At the end of the lower sixth I achieved 2 more 'O' Levels in History (grade B) and General Studies (grade B). Notice the exams I passed I achieved grade Bs! What it clearly proved and demonstrated was that I had the ability and with confidence and belief anything was possible. The point I am trying to make is that many kids I knew were under so much pressure to become doctors or dentists that they overlooked what they were good at and chose all science subjects for their options. This was my mistake. If only parents understood that there are so many professions that your kids can go into. Don't pressure them with your ideology of success. Spend time with your kids understanding what makes them tick. Realising I am an arts based person, I really enjoyed studying History and Sociology. The point is I passed my 'A' Levels and eventually achieved the required number of 'O' Levels. The grades were good enough to study Law at East Anglia. My parents, as you would expect, were overjoyed. Their son was a lawyer before I had even set foot in the Essex countryside. Life couldn't be much better, or could it, as I was about to find out.

TEENAGE KICKS

It was the beginning of my upper sixth that I was to meet a friend who would become like a brother to me. Bally Sonsoiy attended President Kennedy School at the same time as me, even though we never really hung out together. However it was almost six years later that we became great pals. After leaving President Kennedy school, Bally attended Stoke Park School sixth form. Like myself, he had not passed that many 'O' levels and had to retake his exams. Bally lived around the corner from me at Leyburn Close. On the opening day of the Upper Sixth, Bally happened to see me on my way to school and we both just walked up together. A chance meeting that turned into a lifetime friendship. Unbeknown to me he had passed his 'O' levels and was to complete his 'A' Levels at Kennedy. He was a decent lad and, with the sixth form becoming much smaller in numbers, it was easier to become friends with everyone. For some reason Bally and I just hit it off from the start. Bearing in mind we were never really friends for six years, it did seem strange to suddenly act as though we had been pals for years.

Besides living nearby we had similar cultural backgrounds and both our fathers were strict. To be fair to my dad, I would go as far to say that Bally's dad was a couple of notches stricter. I remember him telling us of an incident where he was innocently having a chat with a fellow student who happened to be female. His father somehow must have seen them and what followed was unbelievable. Out of nowhere his father appeared with a knife and chased Bally down Dunster Place threatening to chop off his crown jewels. Luckily he never got near Bally, though I was told it was a close call on all counts. The next day Bally explained that his father thought he was courting this girl. In reality we were both starved of excitement and this happens when you have strict fathers. You just want to see how far you can go without getting caught.

Bally passed his driving test as soon as he turned 17. I was still in the process of learning. I started to have driving lessons after school and must have mustered about seven lessons when I felt I could drive adequately. The driving instructor obviously thought not. Bally, feeling like he was a lady's man, began taking his dad's car to school. He would disconnect the mileage wire so his father would not find out and we would both enjoy the journey to school. Just taking a car to school gives you a sense of empowerment. Confidence was so sky high that on some occasions I would drive the car to school without a licence and insurance. A stupid thing to do, I know, but when you are growing up it's the last thing on your mind. You literally think you are invincible. There was also a great feeling taking the car through the school gates. You were an adult and suddenly other kids wanted to be like you, or so I thought. I did have some near misses when showing off to one particular girl, when I nearly knocked a student over. Luckily for me the tyre went over his foot. Fortunately his brother was a great mate and stopped his kid brother from complaining to the teachers. He did have to make the story up when he went home as his foot had swelled and he was struggling to walk. He was off school for a week so he did benefit from my driving! It was also during this time we both decided to make a visit to Park Lane nightclub in Coventry. There was absolutely no way our parents would let us go, but the excitement of going to a club was too much. It was also becoming embarrassing that at 18 we had yet to visit a club. On the very few occasions we would go, which would be midweek, I would explain to my parents I was hanging out at Bally's house until late. Watching Bally escape from his house would be more exciting than going to the club. Out of the top window would come his long legs and then like a stuntman he would jump on to the drain pipe and shimmy his way down. How we both never got caught astounds me to this day. Attending nightclubs never did live up to the hype so we stopped visiting, which is fortunate as I am sure it was only a matter of time before we both got caught.

Sixth form has to be my most enjoyable time at school. There was a great group of people that decided to stay on as opposed to go to college. Even in the sixth form there is still a focus and a discipline, whereas you are almost left to your own devices at colleges. The teachers have known you for five years and, while you are granted a degree of freedom, you know how far you can go before you cross the line. With few subjects to study, much more time and effort can be dedicated to your chosen subjects. There is also the security of familiarity which appealed to me. In all honesty I was not ready for college and would have drowned in the mass of students. As I said we had a good mix of people who were honest, hardworking students. From day one I have tended to speak to everyone, but have two or three real friends who you can confide in.

The other point that struck me in the 6th form was the number of Asian kids who stay on. This again is the influence of parents, who are determined to see their children better themselves in a society they see as unequal. As a student growing up your experiences and interactions with teachers can give you a false interpretation of society. On the whole you very rarely hear of a teacher who has been fired for any wrongdoing. You may not like particular teachers, but it never had anything to do with a serious breach of employment.

Unfortunately, all the security of being in cotton wool is eroded the moment you leave school. The real world is not always as imagined. We had some great characters in the 6th form, people such as Mr T, a wannabe actor who was always up for a laugh. I'm not sure where he has ended up but would not be surprised if he is working in Bollywood on some X-rated movies. You had the clever ones such as John Stokes and Peter Bailey. These lads seemed to know it all. They were literally A grade students. Then you had the average category where students would be expected to pass and then move to a mid-table University. There was one final category for those who may get through but nothing guaranteed. That was my category.

In everyone's lives there will be a time when you reminisce about the good days. These are days that flew by. You were enjoying life to the full; it was innocent yet exciting. No money worries, no bills or mortgages to pay, you had a life ahead of you that was going to be fantastic. We all have these dreams at a certain point in our young age. I am not aware of anyone who does not dream. Yet most people by their 30s have forgotten their dreams and are allowing fate to take over. Why have all these dreams vanished in to thin air? Why have people changed? I knew students who you would have guaranteed to become successful beyond their wildest dreams yet they are collecting trolleys in supermarket car parks. Some time ago I met a former student who was highly intelligent and expected to have a successful career in finance. He was in a state and while I recognised him I was unsure after all these years whether to speak to him. For some reason, be it curiosity, I did and it ensued that he could not fit into University life and found studying all too much. He literally gave up. What a waste, I thought. Here's me fighting all my life just to hang onto their coattails at school and suddenly the tide had changed. I was not proud but it made me think how important your mindset is in any walk of life. It's easier said than done, but you have to maintain belief and desire when things are tough. Perhaps trying to keep up and having it tough all my life kept me going. For me, every milestone became a success story, overcoming adversity was a victory.

My two years in the sixth form will always be my most enjoyable time. My final year in the sixth form was even more enjoyable than the lower sixth. With Bally on the scene life felt positive. There were no issues with boys and girls mixing and I became friendly with my future wife to be Sharon. A bubbly, attractive character, I was always afraid to speak to her. To be fair I was always nervous around girls. This one though was different; something I cannot explain but you just know. I can honestly say, hand on heart, that being good friends with Sharon urged me on to do well in my exams. We had this kind of chemistry. Well, I had this chemistry, as I don't think she ever noticed me. To be fair she was way out of my league. Not sure why or how I just felt we were on a similar journey.

Musically, U2 had just released their classic album The Joshua Tree. Each and every song was, in my opinion, perfection. No matter what state of mind I was in there was a song to relate to. U2 and all the other experiences in the sixth form shaped my thoughts and ultimately my future. I have heard several people say certain bands changed their life. Music helped me reach a new level. It was inspirational and pertinent to the changes taking place in my life. Since the early 80s I feel like I have been on a spiritual journey with the band. One particular U2 song, Running to Stand Still, was where I was probably at at the time. Life was becoming exciting, adventurous, a whole new world was about to explode and I was ready for the journey ahead.

This was also the time when we were thinking about which universities to attend. Excited about where we could go, I remember reading the University guide book, almost every day thinking of the different cities I could visit. Obviously Cambridge and Oxford never came into the equation. Thinking about it, neither did the top 50 universities. Teachers never really encouraged us to look at the top universities. Just to get a place in University was seen as an achievement. At my stage in life it was all about getting into University. I wanted to go to London, where the bright lights were. Many ex-students who returned would tell us tales of London and how open and buzzing the place is. I had this image of London as one big family partying all the time. My fixation on London was such that I applied to all London institutions bar one. The one I applied to outside of London was Glasgow. I'm not really sure why. However, they offered me a conditional place and sent me information for an open day. Just getting offers was great, I felt valued. The truth was I was never going to Glasgow to study, though I never would have dreamt up the scenario of me one day living in Glasgow many years later to work for one of the biggest football clubs in the world. The truth is choosing a University and a course is stressful. I was picking the easiest universities to get into, which demonstrated what I thought about my own ability. Quite frankly, I had low expectations of myself and to get into University was the be all and end all. It felt like countdown immediately after Christmas. In a few months' time this group of sixth formers, who had known each other since eleven, or in some cases since primary school, were about to leave and embark on a new journey, a destiny that was for the taking. I don't believe any of us thought about marriage, kids or mortgages. We were far too young, naïve, ambitious and unaware of reality. It's amazing how time catches up on you and these are exactly the conversations you are having with your partner or family today.

I had passed my 'A' Level exams first time around. Now that was an achievement in itself. Unfortunately the grades were too low for some of the universities I had applied to in London. However, one day sat at home I received a call from East Anglia Institute of H.E. stating they were prepared to accept me on to the Law degree course. I accepted immediately, even though I forgot I had applied there as a last resort and had no idea where the place was. It did not matter, as the excitement of leaving Coventry to study in Chelmsford kept me excited over the summer months. I was the man about to hit the big time.

Coming from a very tough working class background, I remember not having a decent pair of jeans as money was always tight. The night before I left for University a close friend of mine came round with a quality pair of jeans I could take with me. Can you imagine that happening now? Kids would not be seen without their designer gear these days. Even my trainers and football boots were hand-me-downs from my older brother. It's not a complaint, it's an observation of the times which nurtures you as a person and teaches you to survive and be streetwise.

I needed to earn some money before I left Coventry, so my auntie managed to find me a monotonous packing job during the summer months. The company was based in Bedworth on the only industrial estate in the village. I was offered the position after a one day trial and thought great, I can earn some good money over the next few months. When my dad asked how much I was being paid, I didn't know what to tell him. Great, I had found myself a job without asking how much I was going to earn. Bedworth was a twenty minute trek from my house and most of the time I travelled by bus. The company itself was a well-run family business. They had contracts to package toys all ready for Christmas. I got on well with the staff, though tended to keep myself to myself. In all honesty the job was boring. I used to find amusing things to do to keep me from losing my sanity and mental wellbeing. Most of the employees were locals and there were many young people working there. I got to know the young lads and really got on with them. I was one of them and, coming from a similar background, I tend to find such people less pretentious.

Life is what you make of it. When you get to know these people they had aspirations like everyone else. They wanted a better life for their families. The only problem is working at such companies is not a skill and the wages will always be minimal. Talking about wages, I was working from 8am until 6pm five days a week. On receiving my first pay packet on Friday afternoon I was really excited, even though I had no idea how much I was earning. Opening that brown envelope gave me a kind of grown-up feeling. Taking the money out I had to look again. It was a measly £25 for 50 hours work per week, 50p per hour! Kids in the Far East were earning more than me. This was taking the piss, literally. Well in the end I decided to stay but let's just say I economised on how many toys I packed per day.

In reality I could not afford to leave my job. My dad was suffering from health issues at the time and the pressure was on my mum to provide for the family. I wanted to do my bit, whatever it may be. I have always maintained that kids from tougher backgrounds go one of two ways. Either they become successful or they end up in dead end jobs with four mouths to feed and a life of misery. The ones that do well do so because they have this innate desire to get more out of life. No matter what hits them or their circumstances, they can visualise a better life. No excuses or anyone to blame. Their destiny is not written by fate. They create their fate. We all have dreams in younger life and want to succeed and be someone. Those dreams, for many, suddenly dissipate with time and age and allow fate to become their master. It should not matter what age anyone is. There are no rules or regulations to stop anyone achieving what they want. Age gives you an advantage. It gives you wisdom and experience. I do wish schools would be less regimented and take the plunge to teach kids survival skills alongside the normal curriculum. Not all kids have the confidence to realise their dreams and, like most, they need support. We all do. I am sure we all know of people who are clever academically yet left school early. Why are kids not coached or supported before and after leaving school? Careers advice in the 80s and 90s was a shambles. I remember during my fifth year having a ten minute consultation with the careers teacher. There was no proper advice and, at that age, few kids really know what they want to do other than leave school.

I am sure there is much more support now, but what of the last generation? I am sure some of those kids could have chosen a better life if only they had the correct support and advice. My dad may not have been educated but he knew from day one that I was never going to go through what he had to, toiling for hours for low wages. That's why he was strict and always pushed me to study. He tried to keep me from distractions and would always warn me about the dangers in life. Education, for him, was the only solution to a better life. As kids, you misread what your parents want or say. It's that rebellious nature of doing what they don't want you to do. When the tide is turned and you become a parent the process starts again. Kids need to be spoken to, encouraged to learn and shown how to bounce back from setbacks. We will all experience some form of knockbacks in life, so prepare the next generation to deal with these issues and give them an outlet to speak or communicate to before it's too late.

GOODBYE COVENTRY

My first year in Chelmsford was an experience. A small town close to London. It was a student town with a few bars and clubs catering for the future of the country. The first few weeks were incredible. I had the freedom to do whatever I wanted. It's strange how excited one feels when you are about to leave home. All the new experiences, as if heaven is literally around the corner. Then reality hits home when life isn't exactly as you thought it would be. Yes, as a student it's a great experience, learning to manage on a pittance which actually was fine for me. Remarkably, when I left University I only had a £200 debt, which felt like a mountain at the time. How times have changed.

I remember my first day at Chelmsford meeting my fellow students. At only 18, the world around me felt peaceful and full of optimism. Chelmsford itself is a beautiful commuter town with a high level of affluence. Being quite a sociable person, I immediately made a number of friends. To be fair University is a great place to socialise, as every first year is in the same boat and is keen to meet fellow students. After a few weeks you begin to form smaller friendships and those who become your trusted colleagues. I felt many of the students were much more mature than me. It's amazing how over a year or two some students become and act like adults. In school most kids cannot wait to leave, yet when you hit the real world you wished you made the best of your school years. Like most things in life, we tend to appreciate the good things in hindsight.

On the first day my brothers dropped me off. I vividly remember sitting on my bed in the halls of residence. If they stayed any longer I was going to burst into tears. Reality had set in that I was hundreds of miles away from home and about to begin a new life.

As with all universities, I arrived during Freshers' Week. This allows students to familiarise themselves with their surroundings and fellow students. It's more like a settling in period. The first evening, a few of us went to the student union bar, allowing us to meet new friends and generally socialise. The union bar was packed due to Freshers' Week. Not being a drinker, I had a shandy which raised some eyebrows. Most students were drinking like old timers but I never really acquired a taste for alcohol until later on in life.

I always remember Chelmsford as a sunny, happy place. They are my memories. Even though I struggled to settle, I still have happy memories of the place. The halls of residence were on Duke Street and consisted of two storey buildings housing up to 8 people. I was fortunate to have some great people in my house that I have now lost complete touch with. The ones who come to mind included Jason from Thanet, Paul from Yorkshire, Carl from Worcester, Russell and Carmen from Ireland, Katie from Somerset, Nick also from Coventry and Mel, who I never go to know, but let's just say was the posh one.

Jason and I became close friends and the fact we were on the same law course helped. He always reminded me of Nigel Havers and had that posh accent that endeared us all to him. Residing in Thanet, I never found out why he supported Wolves, but he was a big Steve Bull fan. Paul, who was my neighbour in the flat, was a broad, chubby lad. He was also one of the popular ones in the house as he had a portable TV. Very few students had TVs. Paul was a good, honest lad who would do anything for anyone. A great storyteller with that typical broad Yorkshire accent, I wish I had stayed in touch with him. Russell the Irishman, as I called him, was also a fun character. He was always up for a laugh and very sincere. He was also very tall, probably 6ft 6 inches. A Jolly Green Giant the girls would call him. Carmen, also from Ireland, was the opposite height of Russell. Almost 4ft would be about right. Carmel was another character who was up for a laugh and one who always appeared to argue with Russell. I am sure they were brother and sister from different mothers.

With my previous experiences, I was conscious of being the only Asian in the house. This was absolutely ludicrous as I was treated brilliantly by all. In some respects I found myself out of my depth when it came to maturity. Even though most students were eighteen, I always feel most Asian kids lag behind when it comes to life after 18. It certainly took me a few years to gain that older maturity feel. It's a hard one to explain.

Another lad I got to know and who became good friends with me was Jonathan, who was from Blackburn. The first time I met him was at the Students' Union bar. He had this presence about him, and being tall certainly helped his cause. The first thing I noticed about him was the smell of strong aftershave. It's as if he had immersed himself in this bottle of Tuscany. We hit it off straight away and the one thing he definitely had going for him was his looks. The girls loved him and for some reason he enjoyed my company, which meant I got to meet some of his admirers. The Students' Union at East Anglia was small and could fit about 200 students at best. The first week was incredible and you did meet many new faces. The thing with students is they are great to meet in the first week. They are in the same boat as you and just as nervous. It's during the next few weeks that the real personalities come out of their shells. That's when groups are formed just like at school.

Everything in life appears to be an extension of school in so many ways. Be it at University or work. During Freshers' Week I was out every night. Socialising and constantly meeting new people, it was great. One of the nights we had a disco and me being me decided I was a good dancer. I had all these dodgy moves, a kind of disco mixed with bhangra. I decided to retire after just one night and thank the Lord we had no mobiles or tablets about. I am sure I would have attracted thousands of Youtube views for the wrong reasons.

The Students' Union did have a good reputation for attracting Indie bands and one of the performances that stood out for me was from Blue Aeroplane. One of the group members just danced all through the set. The dance was peculiar in that he was making these weird and wonderful hand movements. The band wasn't bad either. After the gig, a couple of us ended up in their dressing room. This knocked my illusion about rock bands. I was expecting pissed up blokes with loads of groupies. Instead they were having a civil intellectual conversation with us all and I couldn't quite come to terms with that. Where's all the havoc? Just shows how powerful the media can be in their messaging.

This was also the period when rave parties began springing up everywhere. For me the music during this period was about the Stone Roses, U2, New Order, UB40 and The Charlatans with a bit of bhangra thrown in for good measure. For a few years it appeared the young adult nation had become peace-loving hippies. Football violence was almost non-existent, raves were on the up and people just danced away the night in their own world. There was no hassle at the gigs either.

One particular rave I did go to was mind-blowing. A few friends who knew where and when these parties were going to be took me with them. It was in some old decrepit farm building near London. Out of nowhere all these people turned up dressed in designer gear. I was just in some normal jeans and T-shirt and certainly gave the impression it was my first time. All I can remember is that the music was loud and everyone was dancing. We had a few drinks and I managed to consume a couple of

Red Stripes, nothing too over the top, but enough to give me Dutch courage to talk to people and not be nervous. My dancing as always was shite, but it didn't matter, as everyone around me was spaced out. Being at an all-night party, I was worried as to how I would manage to last the course. Naïve, that was me, but I lasted and let's just say I was flying to the music; I didn't realise Red Stripe could do that! It must have been a special brand of beer as it's never had the same effect since.

Over time I became friends with Simon, who came from East London. For some reason Simon missed out on the halls of residence and was put in a student house. I can categorically state that if I had moved into the house he was in I would have returned home almost immediately. It was hard enough adjusting to being away from home and I was lucky I was surrounded by some great people. His house was a dump and, to make matters worse, was occupied by post-graduate geeks who would complain if he brought back students to the house. Coming from a similar background we gradually gravitated to hanging out more and more. It was my way of forgetting about home. The law course itself was interesting, though I never really gave it a go. As I mentioned before, I was always on edge in Chelmsford.

Duke Street was the one famous street that hosted all the kebab and burger bars. Further down from Duke Street was the only nightclub in town. I remember once making a late night visit to the club during Fresher's Week. This one appeared classier than Park Lane in Coventry. There was a calmer crowd to begin with and I never felt intimidated. Admittedly I never went back as nightclubs don't really do anything for me. For one, you cannot hold a conversation due to the loud music and, secondly, come closing time there are drunk and aggressive people everywhere and taxis are a nightmare to find.

In reality the student life in Chelmsford was enjoyable; I made some great friends and it gave me a new lease of life. Cooking, cleaning, all the things you take for granted. At the same time I was always on edge and never quite settled. It was difficult to explain but I did not feel comfortable being too far away from family. Perhaps I was not mentally mature enough to deal with such situations on my own?

As time went on I found myself struggling with the Law degree. I was missing home and could not focus on the course, which needed more attention than most subjects. The inevitable happened. I failed two of the four exams and had to retake them all in the summer. This just a week after I found out my dad was telling his mates and anyone else in earshot at the local temple that I was going to be a hotshot lawyer. Not only did I have to retake the two I failed, but I had to retake the two I passed. Well guess what – I ended up failing all four. You can imagine the grief that was about to come my way. Perhaps education was not for me; had I overachieved with my 'A' Levels? At times I had the feeling I was constantly punching above my weight. The easy route was to give up and find a less demanding position.

After much soul-searching and trying to assess where I was going, once again I decided to continue with higher education by studying at East London University. As I was part of the Asian generation that was fairly new to attending University, there was not an emphasis on which University to attend as there is now. Just to study at a University back in the 80s was considered an achievement. Only five or ten years earlier the norm was for kids to leave school at 16 and find a suitable apprenticeship. Money was tight and most working class families didn't expect their children to necessarily go to University. That was for the really intelligent kids. I certainly put a stop to that myth! From the 90s onwards

University became more accessible as families from all backgrounds had more disposable income and could afford for their children to study higher education. The government was also paying University fees and offering grants to students for the duration of the degree. In many ways University life is exciting as you meet like-minded people and allows you the freedom to do almost what you want.

The pull for Asian kids to go to University was enormous. University was the only acceptable establishment your parents would happily let you leave home for before marriage. For the kids they could truly find themselves and have the freedom they would never have while living at home. This applied to boys and girls. This also probably explains why a lot of Asian kids have problems when they go to University, as they do not know how to handle the freedom and do more damage in their first year than the rest of their lives. In my particular case I could not handle being away from home. I just could not settle and being so close to my family may have manifested itself in my downfall at East Anglia.

In today's era choosing the right University and course is imperative. The costs involved almost add up to a mortgage. You cannot get away with a soft degree due to the financial implications. A degree needs to lead to a career or a position with opportunities. For me, East London University really was last chance saloon, but now I was studying what I was interested in and not complying with the Asian culture or making others happy. Like most things in life, if you enjoy something the likelihood is you will perform to your best and achieve a desirable outcome. The key to achieving is having belief, persistence and faith.

Back home for the summer, I waited eagerly for my results. Deep down I knew I would struggle to pass, but you still have that faintest hope of somehow getting through. When the results arrived I was disappointed and quite frankly pissed off that no matter what I did I'd have to work even harder to get ahead in life. As mentioned earlier, I failed all my retakes and that had to be one of the lowest points in my life. My mind was confused and I was not thinking straight. Again, I had this overwhelming sense of motivation, which came across me that I must not give up and give it another go with a subject you enjoy. I didn't need any persuasion – I was going to make it; this really was the last roll of the dice. I enrolled at the University of East London on a four year degree studying Social Policy with a strong influence of Psychology. If Chelmsford was an experience, East London was on another level. Fortunately I had some friends from Coventry who were studying here and this time round I actually enjoyed my time. I was much more mature and ready to leave home. I look back on my time in Chelmsford with fond memories. A whipper-snapper who thought he could take on the world coming back home with his tail between his legs. But it was a fantastic experience and one that prepared me for when I studied at East London. Never regret anything; look at life as a positive experience. Difficult as this may sound, try and find positives out of a negative situation. There is no such thing as a failure. They are simply outcomes or responses. Take on your fears and face them head on. There will only be one winner and that's you and your courage.

EAST LONDON –
LAST CHANCE SALOON

East London University was based in Barking and Maryland. Barking was the main campus, where most of the facilities for students were located. Maryland was a much smaller campus and was very tired and old. This was where I was based until the second year onwards. I always had a fascination with London and to finally secure a degree course at East London was a relief. In reality I could have chosen a number of London Universities but at the time I didn't have anybody I could speak to. Careers teachers just wanted you off their stock and didn't appear to be very knowledgeable. To me, East London was as good as any other University and was easier to get into. The truth is I had no idea of University ratings, besides the obvious ones of Cambridge and Oxford. Nowadays students are much more prepared and know almost all there is to know about their chosen University. The league tables highlighted on the website or in any respectable paper make every difference and did not exist to the best of my knowledge during the 80s. Choosing East London University had as much to do with the course I wanted to enrol on as how easy it was to get onto that course. I was also aware of a number of former students from Kennedy who were attending and had only good things to say.

This time I was much more prepared. My first year was spent living in a small room on Western Road, West London. A friend of mine from Coventry was on work experience from East London University at Hammersmith Hospital and, not fancying halls of residence, I agreed to share a house with him. The journey to East London was a round trip of two hours. Luckily the hours at University in the first year were no more than 25 hours of lectures per week and they normally started late morning or early afternoon.

West London also appealed to me, as Central London and all the decent places to eat and drink were a tube ride away. Being much more confident, I made friends quickly from my course and I felt more mature with handling University life. With so much time on my hands I would spend time meeting up with Sharon, who was working in Central London, and going out socially with fellow students. Life as a student was much more enjoyable. I even had dreams of learning to play the guitar and forming my band called Arena Red, a name I wrote on the back of my rucksack at 13 years of age at President Kennedy school. They were simply pipe dreams and something one does when they have too much time on their hands.

London is a fantastic place for students with so many places to socialise. I rarely went out during the week due to financial constraints and even with my grant I was living on just over £50 per week after rent. That included my bills, shopping, travel and going out. It was tough to survive this way, but when you are brought up in a tough environment you learnt to survive and budget accordingly. When you have nothing, you have nothing to lose. Friday nights at Maryland was a must for me. This was alternative music night. Interestingly I was one of a few Asians who used to attend, as the majority of Asians would be found enjoying R&B at Barking Student Union.

During my first year I was also involved with helping a friend arrange bhangra gigs at venues across the country. Attending clubs in different cities and watching established artists perform was exciting. I do enjoy Punjabi music and it was bands such as DCS and Alaap that first got me interested. I have diverse music tastes and enjoy several genres of music. Due to my older brother's influence, I have grown up on English and Punjabi music. For those who know of bhangra music, it has its place but listening to it first thing in the morning can be explosive. Surely not for the faint hearted when the beats start rolling.

Some of the more notable gigs I attended were at the Hammersmith Palais, Watford's Paradise Lost, Bradford Maestro and Fox's nightclub in Wolverhampton. The gig in Wolverhampton was eventful for all the wrong reasons. The organiser, who has to be one of the best young entrepreneurs I had the pleasure to work with, had a disagreement with the security team he normally hired. For this particular event he paid some big lads who worked with his brother and other people he knew. Hiring people because of their build is one thing, but they were not bouncers or had any previous experience with crowd control. On this particular gig M needed help with collecting money from customers. I offered and took my position in the booth. Unbeknown to me the security team M allegedly had a problem with arrived at the gig. The first thing they did was to head to the booth I was standing in. Let's just say I agreed when they asked to enter the booth where the night's takings were. My life was too precious to be messing about with these guys. On finding out, M notified his so-called hired bouncers. They did go out to see the commotion and then made a run for it when confronted by the security firm. After the incident M decided to leave the scene due to the stress it caused him and his family. For days after I remember M telling me how he and his brother kept a shotgun at home in fear of further reprisals. Fortunately there were no further issues, and I believe M has since moved abroad.

Once M was off the scene I decided to focus much more on my University life. Bhangra gigs in the 80s and 90s were popular among Asian students, as they could attend without their parents knowing. Many were organised by their student union societies. It was the place to meet other students and friends. Remember social media did not exist. There were no mobile phones, twitter or Facebook. If you wanted to socialise you went out. Gigs really became a huge phenomena during the early 90s. Many bands were only too pleased to be on the bill. You could organise bhangra gigs with five well known artists for less than £5,000 and that included the venue. During this period M was earning in excess of £4,000 per gig, and this while he was at school studying for his 'A' Levels. Over 90% of M's gigs were sold out. I also learned a great deal about marketing and negotiating while spending time with M.

On one particular occasion we nearly got arrested for fly posting in Southall. The gig at Hammersmith Palais was only a few weeks away and M wanted to ensure the venue was full to capacity. Southall, West London was where the first wave of Asian immigrants settled during the 60s and 70s. A culturally diverse area, many Asians bought shops and opened various businesses catering for the local community. It was like mini Punjab. There were suit shops for women, a range of Indian fast food outlets, jewellers and music shops. Even during the week the main parade was buzzing with people, music and the smell of Indian cuisine. Even as an Asian, visiting Southall was an experience in itself; it was like being abroad minus the weather. This was the area M wanted to concentrate on. One of his artists, the lead singer from Alaap, also lived in the area so it made sense to attract the local young adults. I remember visiting the singer one evening with M to sign a contract. While an exaggeration, it's like going to meet Bono from U2 at his house for tea and then asking him if he wants to play a gig in a few weeks time for a couple of hundred pounds, cash in hand.

Late at night we drove around until we found buildings adorned with all types of advertising. A quick brush of glue on the back of the poster and then another person would quickly put the poster up. We found a few places to advertise when suddenly out of nowhere we were being pursued by blue flashing lights. It was the police. The four of us were asked to get out of the car for questioning. Suddenly three other police cars and a riot van arrived. At this stage I was beginning to worry, as I had heard all number of stories about police brutality. Were we about to be framed? So much was racing through my mind. What if I am falsely convicted and have to give up at University? What if my dad finds out? The list was endless and I was running scared. That was until one particular police officer who sensed the atmosphere came up to us and said not to worry, the riot van happened to be in the area. Looking at the four of us we couldn't riot if we were paid to. We were just four normal lads who had never been in trouble with the law. Just before we were summoned out of the car M told us all to give false names if asked. I had to keep myself from laughing when the others gave their names. One was Amitabh Bachchan, the other Dhamendra. Bollywood fans would know of these names as very famous actors in the Indian film industry. It's like being in India and telling the local constabulary you are Mel Gibson and Sylvestor Stallone. To be fair this was a routine check. Admittedly it was a routine check that knocked us for six. We got out of Southall as quick as possible. Can you imagine Amitabh Bachchan and Dhamendra on the front pages of the Southall news, caught fly posting in an old Fiesta?

Looking back, we were just young lads finding our way in life. University not only plays a critical role in education, it also enables young students to learn the harsh realities of life. You are playing out adulthood before life has even begun. There are financial management lessons to deal with, notably rent, bills, weekly food shopping and keeping enough aside for the weekend. Most students I knew could manage on their grants during term time and worked during the summer months to prevent them from being overdrawn. I always had a job lined up each summer to tide me over.

I moved to East London from my second year onwards and lived at Hampton Road, Ilford. It was a solid terraced house and very spacious. The rent was affordable at only £45 per week and was only a twenty minute walk from the University. Jonathan, who was one of my flatmates, was on the same course as me and we had many memorable evenings debating life and putting the world to rights long into the early hours.

Ilford is a vibrant area of East London, with a host of nationalities merged with a large student population. In many ways I viewed Ilford as a mini Southall. The main Ilford Road was dominated by Asian owned shops and restaurants. As a student Ilford was great for food, affordable housing and a tube ride away from the bright lights of Central London. It was also an area where you had to be on guard and have your wits about you. There were a number of stabbings and muggings while I was there during the early nineties. Fortunately I never heard of any students encountering any problems. For any social evenings we would all go out as one large group. Mugging a student would probably be a bad idea as we could just about muster a few pounds at the best of times. I also noticed very few students had cars and most would use public transport or walk to their destination.

I treated University as an extension of the sixth form, albeit with all the freedom in the world. I remained focussed and disciplined on my work, and only ever requested an extension to a project once in four years. This was also the time I began writing poetry during my free time. Poetry allows you to express yourself and convey your feelings in that particular moment. It was a release mechanism and also served to allow me to dream about whatever I wanted to. There was no thought control or any ideology to succumb to. The freedom to think and act is a powerful tool we all take for granted. As someone once said to me, if you had no fear what would you do? The list was endless, but then so was the fear.

My challenge was to dispel the thought of fear and doubt and continue my journey to achieve something good in life, whatever that may be. I had knockbacks growing up but the one positive side I possessed in abundance was never to give up; no matter how many times I was thrown to the floor I would keep getting up. Life is about setbacks and knockdowns and, for me, this was a challenge. Later on in life I realised pressure brought the best out of me. As soon as the shit hit the fan I was on to it, ready to make a plan work. I was enjoying my student life at East London University. I also made more of travelling into Central London to enjoy the buzz of being in the heart of the capital. As a group of friends, we would take time out on the weekends to take a walk in Hyde Park, enjoy the opulence of Harrods and then take in a film at Whiteleys in Bayswater. Central London just had this aura that attracted me to the place regularly. Other times we would just take a tube ride to different areas just for the fun of it. During the spring times I would often make a trip to Camden market, which had a Bohemian presence. I could never grow tired of London and it will always have a special place in my heart. London is an inspirational city which gave me the visceral courage to keep going and never give up.

I had made some great friends and was enjoying my degree course, which always helps. My third year started off well as I began choosing my modules and my work placement. I found a place to live near the University and I started to feel my life was starting to take shape. It was not long before I would graduate and begin a career. It was during my third year that a horrific incident left an indelible mark on my life. One late evening I received a call from Sharon, asking if I could accompany her and a friend to an incident her sister had been involved in. The call was vague and at this point it did not appear to be serious. The incident in question was in Nottingham and being so late they wanted me to accompany them. Apparently Sharon's sister had been involved in an accident and at this point the details were minimal, though we thought nothing more of it. We all met at Sharon sister's house and waited for further details. At this stage nobody seemed panicked other than what her parents would have to say if there were injuries. After some calls to the house we were told the accident was much more serious and that we should go and see her sister immediately. Even at this stage we were not overly concerned. We must have left East London at approximately 11pm. This was going to be one long journey. Once we reached the outskirts of Nottingham we stopped at the service station to check which hospital Sharon's sister was taken to. I was volunteered to make the call. Once I had given my details to the nurse, a fellow student, who was also involved in the accident, appeared on the other end of the phone. What she said to me in the next few seconds left me numb, devastated and speechless. At first I did not comprehend what was being said to me and kept asking how Sharon's sister Aman was. It was the silence on the other side of the phone that then hit me and sunk in exactly what we were dealing with. I put the phone down and looked at both Sharon and her friend and just said which hospital we should attend. I could not tell them the truth. I could not accept the truth.

During the short drive to the hospital I will never forget the Duran Duran song Ordinary Day being played on the radio. The eerie music and lyrics just went with the atmosphere. It took me over 15 years before I could listen to that song again. Once we arrived at the hospital we were met by a nurse at reception. The look on her face said it all, but I also knew the truth. The next few seconds were about to change a family's life. The nurse explained Aman had been in an accident and unfortunately had not survived. Even at this stage Sharon asked the nurse again how her sister was and whether she could see her. The silence said it all and Sharon just went into profound thought. We eventually made our way back to Coventry to drop Sharon off at her parents' home. Even to this day I cannot imagine the deep sadness the family must have gone through of losing a daughter so young. The journey back to London felt like a lifetime. What made the situation even more difficult was trying to understand the circumstances surrounding the accident. What the family were being told just did not appear to add up. They say time is a healer, though I do not believe Aman's mother and father will ever overcome the grief of losing their daughter so young and in such tragic circumstances.

Sharon eventually returned to University. For the sake of her younger sisters she showed incredible courage and bravery to keep the family intact and kept going to give them a better life. No doubt she took the punches. That day I made a personal pledge to support Sharon and give her the best possible life I could. I was prepared to do whatever it took to ensure no harm ever came over her. Every person deserves happiness in this world. Spiritually I felt it was my duty to do whatever I could to help. The end of my third and penultimate year at University can best be summed up as a time of melancholy.

Before my final year commenced, one of my good friends on the course, Vic, asked if I wanted to live with him and his friends as they had a spare room. This was ideal for me as they were all in their final year at University and I needed the space and more importantly few distractions. Being in the final year was a relief as I wanted to finish as soon as possible and proceed with a career. I certainly had my fair share of University life. The house I rented was on Mortlake Road, a 15 minute walk to campus. I was determined to study even harder and achieve a good result. After several false dawns and what felt like a lifetime of studying, my time had arrived. A few more months and I would have that coveted degree I so wanted. All that pain, heartache and playing with my mind as to whether I was cut out for studying or not was about to become a reality.

The year passed by peacefully though, as usual, I had the odd issue, such as our next door neighbours. They were friends of our landlord. What Vic failed to explain before I moved in was we had to whisper after 9pm as the walls were wafer-thin and the neighbour would get agitated by the sound of voices. Surely this was a laugh and I was having none of it. One evening after moving in to the house we had friends around. We were just talking when the phone rang. Paz, one of my housemates, took the call and then told us we needed to be quiet as the neighbour had called saying we were too noisy. This occurred regularly and my housemates just lived with the situation. After a few weeks I got absolutely pissed off with the neighbour's antics. This was our house, and he had no right to tell us what time we could talk until. If we had regular parties or played loud music I could understand, but he was becoming a maniac and I wasn't standing for it. One night I completely lost it with this idiot. We had just returned from the Student

Union bar and, like most students, were chatting away, nothing too loud, when suddenly the phone rang. He was ranting and raving about the noise level. I'm not sure what happened but I blew my fuse, which is unlike me, and I started shouting back and gave him a few home truths. Suddenly it all went quiet. That's done the trick, I thought to myself, no more phone calls.

Twenty minutes later there was banging at the front door. Vic looked out of his bedroom window and then shouted it's the police and dived for cover on the landing. Vic was sprawled all over the floor as if a grenade had just been thrown through the window. It almost became a Monty Python sketch. Why are you diving for cover, we all enquired, as if we were about to be attacked by the SAS? He just looked up at us and said there are loads of them and riot vans. Ash, the sensible one, was voted by us all to open the door. At this point we were not really worried about his welfare; we were too busy thinking about our own situation. On opening the door the sergeant looked at him and asked where's the party? Ash just stared at the officer and said you must have the wrong address. No, I have been told there is a house party that is causing a nuisance to the neighbours and this is the address I have. Look around, said Ash, there's only four of us and certainly no party. The officer was not happy having to bring out the full East London riot squad only to find four skinny, harmless, shit-scared students staring back at him. The officer even apologised for waking us up. I'm not sure what happened to the neighbour but he never called us again.

Completing the final exams was like a burden off my shoulders. It was total relief. I knew I had gained a degree, it was the result that now mattered. I was a borderline 2:1. What a result if I finished with a 2:1! The only piece of work standing in the way of my 2:1 was the dissertation. Any student will tell you the dissertation is the one final piece of the jigsaw that can knock the shit out of anyone. The constant research, travelling to different specialised libraries; it's full on. Even the party animals suddenly become studious and realise they need to put some effort in. It's like your whole University life rests on this one huge, gigantic piece of work. The previous years become a distant memory. A piece of advice – choose a topic or theme that will keep you interested for more than a week. I only went and picked a crap topic for my dissertation, which became so boring I lost interest. I was so far down the line with the dissertation that I could not change the theme. In the end I just wanted to hand in whatever it was and hoped for the best.

After four years of studying I eventually graduated with a 2:2 honours degree, a proud moment in my life. I was proud, because I had beaten all the adversity and all the negativity that I was not good enough to study. Years of underachieving had finally come to an end. In retrospect I had planted a seed in my mind that I will achieve a degree. I never gave up as I knew I would succeed. Through hard work and travelling in different directions and making serious decisions which meant losing certain friends who were a negative influence, I finally achieved the first goal I set out to gain. If I can, anyone can. My degree was varied and not specific to an industry. Was this a good thing or not? Well, at the time I didn't care. In all honesty I just wanted to complete my degree and then see where I went from there. I had no preference to what I wanted to do. I actually didn't know what was out there. Unlike today, where we have social media and properly informed careers teachers, my knowledge was limited. What I did feel was a sense of excitement of taking on the world. I have always been a dreamer and constantly visualise the future. This is what keeps me motivated and driven. I always had a reason to progress; it was my question of the WHY? that kept me going even when I was faced with challenging issues. The question of why is key to any person's development and progression. In my opinion unless you have a burning desire to achieve a task it will eventually fizzle out and you will find yourself back to square one. Life in general is one huge journey that you can dictate to or be dictated at. From early school age we are dictated to. We have to learn to live among our community, we learn right from wrong. At a certain point in life you have to take the plunge. Push yourself to go further and take risks which will eventually provide you with a new road. This is your road and you can walk it as and when you want. It's yours for the taking.

NO MONEY, NO JOB, NO INTERVIEWS

My next goal was to find suitable employment. Unfortunately, in the Asian culture, being on the dole has a stigma attached. You have to work. To make matters worse, I actually wanted some time out to reflect on my success. To many with a degree it's a means to an end. For me it was worth rejoicing, it was a huge achievement. One month became two months and suddenly the pressure was on to find a job. Living at home was a bit of an issue as I had to change back to my dad's rules of getting up early and spending the day looking for suitable employment. He didn't quite get it that I was 24 and not a child. When you have lived a life of freedom for six or seven years and suddenly you are living under strict rules the word oppression comes to mind. There was even a curfew on what time I could watch TV until late at night, as it may affect my job prospects!

To make matters worse, I had told my parents about Sharon, my future wife who I had studied with at University. The first thing they enquired about was religion and caste. That was fine, but then they wanted to know what village her family resided from in India. Village, why, do you want to research the family tree in some remote village in Punjab? The reason was in case we were related. Obviously we were not related in any shape or form; my next door neighbour could have told them that! The marriage could go ahead. Well, it wasn't as straightforward as that. It appeared we needed some middle man to broker the deal. So the parents of a close friend of mine agreed to become the middlemen and approached the girl's side of the family to explain we have a lad who has a degree (let's not forget the degree). All was well until they started enquiring in which subject.

Well, that's the next problem – I had to explain what my degree constituted of to the middlemen who just nodded their heads with a conspicuous smile, probably thinking what sort of fucking degree is that? He's not a doctor, dentist or an accountant, but some unemployed social worker. On the second visit they brought a professional, a proper veteran in brokering marriage deals. I was asked a whole host of questions, mainly about me being unemployed and how I would look after their daughter. At one stage I am sure they must have been thinking their daughter could do better than this. Sharon was probably grilled and shown a list of eligible doctors, accountants and dentists she could choose from rather than opt for this unemployed Delboy.

The pressure was on. I had to find a job. I spent months sending my CV to local firms. I even wore my out of date suit and walked round different firms personally handing out my CV. They took my CV, probably out of sympathy, but gave me strange looks. On one occasion a charming lady even said she had no change to give me but to try the local YMCA. I only wanted to hand in my CV but perhaps I was becoming a charity case. I registered with agencies. I made friends with the recruiters; everything that made me appear desperate. Desperate I was. On another occasion a local recruitment firm in Coventry sent me to a company in Rugby for a telesales role. Was this my big break? I looked the part and smelt nice with a splash of aftershave. Once I arrived some lady showed me around – to this day I am still not sure what the job was selling but I did everything I could to get the job. I was confident, probably too confident, but I needed a job and was prepared to do anything for a break. The big question came at the end – do you have any experience? No, but I can learn.

By the time I got back to the recruitment agency things turned sour. I remember walking in to the agency and heading to the recruitment consultant. He looked at me and said the company had complained for sending me, as I had no experience. Why didn't you tell them? It then came down to something more sinister. He said they didn't want an Asian employee. I just looked at him and said, you're taking the piss, this is the mid 90s not the mid 60s. True or not that was his excuse. Ironically I was told of a recruitment consultancy position that was about to be advertised at this particular recruitment firm. Naturally I applied. The first part of the interview process was to undertake a series of psychometric tests. If I passed the test I would be offered an interview with the Senior Manager. Well I failed the psychometric test and remember one of the managers explaining the process. For me they were just a series of questions and I was told there is no right or wrong answer. In all my time I have never believed in such tests. They do not explain your personality or how creative you are; they are too scientific for my liking. I am sure psychometric tests have their place, just not in my home! I was back to the drawing board.

I had no money, no job, no career and no interviews. To top it all I was getting married in less than a year and we had no money to fund the wedding – to say I was well and truly screwed was an understatement.

No matter how motivated a person is it is times like these that you start questioning yourself. Self doubt begins to creep in. After a period of feeling sorry for myself I would try and pick myself up again and not let fear rule my world. I never gave up my spirituality which, combined with belief, persistence and faith, was a powerful combination. To pass the time on the dole I would visit a good family friend of ours known as Michael, who was always willing to help and support in any way he could. Some days we would just sit and talk for hours about life. Other times I would hang out in the infamous Bernie's shop, as it was termed by the regulars. Located on Compton Road, Coventry, there was a parade of shops that once flourished. Due to the recession in the 80s many of the stores were closed and boarded up. The landlord, desperate to get something opened, offered Bernie an opportunity to open a games shop for free. Now Bernie was no normal character. A family friend, you would think butter wouldn't melt in his mouth. He became a Holbrook legend for his bravery. In one particular incident Bernie, a larger than life character, became embroiled in a religious situation. Being involved with a local temple, a dispute developed leading to two groups vying for control of the temple. Eventually this led to a high-profile court case in London determining who would gain total control. What should have been a civilised matter in the courts descended into chaos at the motorway service. The opposition group brought in lads from other towns and cities. Not knowing this, Bernie's group was a mixture of young and older folk including pensioners from Coventry. By coincidence the two groups happened to stop for a comfort break at the same service station. Well, as I said previously, Sikhs don't need an excuse for a battle. All hell broke loose. Old men chasing each other with hammers and any weapon they could find. Men, young and old, flying over the racks in WHSmith. They obviously didn't legislate for Bernie. One of the opposition lads must have taken liberties with an older gentleman accompanying Bernie. After giving the so-called fighter a few slaps, Bernie decided to go for the jugular and pulled out his ceremonial sword and chased the lad down the M1 with cars and lorries swerving all over the lanes. This really was one hell of a sight to see. The incident hit the headlines and the national news. The incident was featured on the front page of the Coventry Telegraph. These were not football hooligans but respected men having a riotous day out.

It's obviously in the blood.

Bernie's shop finally opened. It had three slot machines, a pool table and really was a poor excuse for a youth club. Kids from all over the area descended into the shop. All types of characters would visit the place. However, Bernie never once had to control or throw anybody out. He was a legend with a fierce reputation. I spent so much time in Bernie's shop from dawn to dusk. There was nothing else to do. This place gave me some sort of solace from the real world. I knew it was only temporary, but sometimes you need to get away from the harsh realities of life. It was my time out venue. Bernie made several attempts to be entrepreneurial and even allowed the first person each morning to play a free round of pool. Unfortunately, no matter how hard me and my brother Sonny tried, Five Bellies would be there shivering outside the shop just to get his free round of pool. This guy must have literally slept outside the shop. The regulars included Rick the mechanic, who I never witnessed working on a car, and J the taxi driver, who I never saw take a fare. J was easily recognisable as he could never pronounce his H's and you had to concentrate just to understand his English. We also had our very own wannabe master chef who would make us chicken curry at the back of the shop at weekends. In all honesty he could just about muster beans on toast but nobody complained. Saturday was our special night. Everyone would chip in £2 for a chicken curry. The meat was grossly over spiced and tasteless but when you are on the dole you want your two pounds worth. Needless to say the next day was a bummer for many and you could tell on the faces when many were off to see their GP!

In all fairness the shop served a fundamental purpose. It kept the kids off the streets. Parents knew where their kids were and, more importantly, the shop was a mixture of black, white and Asian kids all socialising together.

Closing time was when the last person left. Even Bally completed his Masters degree at the premises. So often he would be writing essays at the back of the shop under extremely smoky conditions. Unfortunately a good thing can sometimes manifest itself into something else. The crime rate in the immediate vicinity shot up and, at times, during the afternoon people would turn up with brand new items to sell. As you can imagine, the goods had no guarantee or a returns policy. However, I need to stress the point that nobody in the shop ever bought any of the goods, impossible as it may be to believe. It is so easy to stereotype people and the learning curve, for me, is not to judge anyone until you get to know them. We did not know the characters and they were discouraged from returning; not in our area and not on our doorstep. Life was bearable but I needed and wanted more. I had to find a job and quick.

One afternoon Michael and I went for a drive for no apparent reason other than to get out of the house. For some reason we travelled past Highfield Road. Coventry City were playing Norwich that day and we must have passed the ground half way through the match. As we passed Michael turned to me and said why don't you work for Coventry City? This was a club that was my life. I was brought up Sky Blue. My first football kit was the infamous chocolate brown kit. When younger I was adamant I wanted the new sky blue striped kit. My older brother and I went around all the sports shops in Coventry trying to find the home sky blue kit but to no avail. In the end I settled for the chocolate kit, as I was desperate to emulate my heroes when playing in the school playgrounds. One week it would be Ian Wallace, the next Mark Hateley and then Garry Thompson. Looking back, I must have looked naked with two white stripes painted down the side of my body. Nevertheless, I was proud to own a kit that has now gone down in folklore as the worst kit ever to be worn by a team in Britain, if not the world. I remember my first game in 1983 watching the Sky Blues play QPR and we won 1-0 with a Dave Bamber goal. That season I must have gone to 90% of the home matches. The highlight that season was beating the mighty Liverpool 4-0 with a Terry Gibson hatrick – quality.

Michael's words struck a chord and kept bothering me for days. Was this an omen? Eventually I persuaded my brother Sonny to write a letter to Bryan Richardson, the Coventry Chairman at the time. It was a truly well-written letter that only he could do. However with the amount of knockbacks I had I wasn't sure what to think, but it was exciting just writing to the Chairman of Coventry City. Two weeks prior to Christmas I received a letter from Coventry City F.C. I opened the letter so slowly, enjoying the moment before being knocked back again. I read it once, twice and again for a third time. It was a message from Bryan's PA, Lesley Brooks, asking me to call back in the New Year as the Chairman has agreed to see me. What a great Christmas I had – just the break I needed.

In the New Year I called Lesley, and we arranged a suitable time and date. On the day of the meeting I was smartly dressed. I always remember my dad telling me the sign of a man is to wear a smart suit, quality shoes and a good watch. Well, one out of three wasn't bad! I had an out of date Casio digital watch and a retro suit, a throwback to the early 80s, but I am sure Bryan had better things to think about. On the morning I remember Lesley meeting me in reception and stating that I had fifteen minutes – for a break like this five will do, I thought to myself.

I was taken to Bryan's office, a large room overpowered

by an oak panelled desk. Bryan had this aura about him similar to a senior government figure. He was well spoken and very inquisitive. After I sat down he said what can I do for you? I want a job, was the reply, and I stacked the rejection letters on his table and said they have lost millions for not taking me on. What do you mean, he asked intrigued? Well, if they had offered me a job I would have made them millions. They are not rejections but responses, he retorted, something that I never forgot. He was a very positive person that resonated with me. What can you do? From the start I have always remained honest and mentioned that I had no experience but what chance did I have to prove myself if no one is prepared to offer me an opportunity. In a last act of desperation I explained he had some great facilities and that he needed someone like me to sell them for him. I was his saviour; through me he was going to make millions. He sat for a while in profound thought. Here we go again, I thought, you are a nice guy etc but we have no jobs. Then he called the Sales Director to see what I could do. I remember the Sales Director sitting uneasy telling me they have no positions. He started questioning me about my experience and me repeating myself I have no experience but!! Have you ever sold on the phone? The questions came flying out. At times he was just going through the motions.

Great, I thought, at least I have spoken to the Chairman of Coventry City Football Club. My dad, who was waiting in the car, looked at me with eager anticipation and waiting for me to say great I've got a job. Not quite, there are no jobs. Back to the drawing board and the job shop I thought.

The dole office started sending me to a job club in Jubilee Crescent. It was bad enough feeling low looking for a job, but having to go to the job shop just made matters worse. This place was even more dull than a doctor's surgery. Two weeks later the Sales Director, who I will refer to as J, calls me and asks me to meet him again. Now there was some hope; surely I had a chance. Again I remained positive. I genuinely believed this was the start of my future. J made it clear again there are no positions, but I could work as a junior telesales for £8k per year. I didn't need any persuasion; I said I'll take the job. I wanted to work and this was my opportunity. J was shocked and said you sure you want to work for £8k per year? Absolutely, at the moment I am on £35 per week, you do the maths pal. He looked shocked, though somehow I knew he had been told to hire me. Not only had I managed to find full time work, I was about to live the dream working for my hometown club.

COVENTRY CITY FOOTBALL CLUB – LIVING THE DREAM

The first day was quite surreal. Being taken on a tour of the ground was incredible, especially when you are a huge fan. The one memory I have is going into the changing rooms and touching the clothes hooks and doors as if they were the crown jewels. It may sound strange but this is where my heroes got changed on match days. The home dressing room was large and square. The next room had two huge bath tubs with just one bath and four showers. With newly built stadiums I am not sure we will ever see the bath tubs where all the players would jump in after a game. The away dressing room was smaller in comparison with a large overbearing cracked mirror right opposite where the players got changed. There were three showers though only two ever worked. However some of the star players and teams such as the Liverpool and Manchester United greats had been here. The list is endless. It's amazing how even empty dressing rooms can take you back to the past, as if you are sat amongst the greats. The boardroom was spectacular, oak panelled tables with big wooden chairs. It actually epitomised everything I would think a boardroom should look like. Steeped in history, this is where the late Derrick Robins and Jimmy Hill would make their decisions. I was about to embark on a journey that would see me progress through the ranks. What I didn't envisage was remaining at the club for almost 14 seasons!

My first role was literally picking up the phone and calling new businesses from 9.00am until 5.00pm. I would be in for 8.15am and not leave until after 6.00pm. Whilst I was the so-called junior I was prepared to work the same times as the Sales Director and my colleagues and most often much longer. Equally, I find it difficult to comprehend when new employees fresh out of College or University begin their new positions yet only work the hours in their contract and then wonder why they fail to progress. There have been several occasions I can recall employing new recruits, some out of University and some moving on from other employment. I can count on one hand the number that would work beyond the call of duty. By this I don't mean having to work long hours to prove your dedication. There are times when you know going that extra mile will not only push that sale over the line but also create fresh new ideas in the process, and this may mean arriving early or staying until late. I am not one to criticise my staff if they arrive at 9am and leave at 5pm. If they complete the tasks expected that's fine. But don't expect promotion or progress if you are not prepared to go the extra mile. This is the life and society we live in. You have a choice.

Working until late was when my creative mind would go into overdrive. During work hours you have so many distractions. After work it's your time and this can be powerful in many ways. The energy can be contagious if your team has the desire, belief and faith to succeed. Feeling a sense of fortune for having this job there was absolutely no way I was going to lose what I had. I was in for the long haul.

The first few weeks calling new businesses was difficult; no training, no planning, actually no structure. The Sales Director and my colleagues were not experts either. We were all in the same boat. To be honest I made it up as I went along. The advantage I had was I knew the club, being a supporter, and so could hold a conversation on the club. I also realised many businesses had never received a call from Coventry City. The commercial department were reactive and literally order takers which, to a degree, you can be in the Premiership. This worked in my favour as I began to sell for both the conference and commercial departments.

The first few months were extremely difficult. The sales and conference department was new and budgets seemed to be made up with what the club was expecting as opposed to realistically what it could achieve. Calling day in and day out does take its toll and at times I absolutely hated it. In hindsight, the difficult years trying to sell on the phones made me what I am today. I learnt so many techniques and how to capture a new customer on the phone. However, for me, I was just happy to be working and more importantly to be earning a wage. In a strange way I was motivated and confident about my future, even though I did not know what was in store. It was a feeling that I got, something I get in life when I believe something good is about to happen. It is with me to this day.

During the first six months we continued to miss the monthly budget. The pressure was on J, who in turn turned the screw on me and my colleague. As time went on I noticed a change in J's attitude as he started to use tough tactics to get what he wanted from me. At first I let it go, apprehensive to say anything due to a fear of losing my job. It's only words, I used to think to myself. I became resilient and would try and just make sense of the situation. J was under extreme pressure to deliver and having a go at his colleagues appeared to be his outlet. This didn't make it right but Wendy, my colleague, and I dealt with it best we could. One day things turned for the worse. The bullying intensified; I had to remain calm and not let it get to me. Unfortunately it's hard not to let something so unsavoury affect you. It was day in, day out. It started to affect my home life. Rather than complain I kept going. In retrospect this was the wrong decision, though in difficult circumstances you go to any lengths if it means protecting your position. Jobs were hard to come by and I decided to take the criticism. In any other situation I would have confronted J and had it out whatever the consequences. Then one day it all just got to me. I couldn't take it any more and remember staring into space at home speaking to myself and asking for help from the Lord, my life was a misery. I felt I had no way out; now I needed help desperately. One day out of the blue the Vice Chairman Mike McGinnity summoned J for a meeting due to not hitting targets. I am not sure what was said but you didn't need to be a genius to know he had received a rollocking. He decided to give me and my colleague the verbal abuse again, blaming us for the lack of business. This is a guy who was earning a fortune compared to me yet never made a call or even brought any business in to the club. To make matters worse, I remember we were in a relegation dogfight (nothing unusual for CCFC) and playing Liverpool that week. J turned around to me and said Coventry will get battered, which really annoyed me. Here is an employee who cannot even support the club that is feeding him. To make matters worse he turned out to be a fan of one our local rivals. Well I had an issue with him making derogatory remarks about our club. As time went on his attitude got worse until it came to a head and I had to have time out from the building to get myself together. This was not what I had signed up to, bearing in mind I was on shit wages. Was work really like this?

Enter the moment I met with Vice President and stalwart of the club – Joe Elliott. Over the years we have become very close friends and share the same passion for our beloved Sky Blues. Joe became aware of the situation with J and assured me this would not continue. Well it didn't. A few days later my colleague and I received a call from Mike McGinnity to meet him in the CCFC offices.

Surely we are not in deep shit, we kept asking ourselves. Perhaps they are closing the department due to poor sales. The meeting was short and simple. From now on no more issues – J is out. That was it, J was leaving and the next day me and my colleague Wendy were taking over. To be fair Wendy and I requested to be given a chance to turn the department around. Being a fair man Mike gave us 6 months. Wendy became the Sales Manager and me, well, I got rid of the title junior – it was a start I guess. We all agreed that if we began making a profit Wendy and I would have an increase in wages. The challenge was on.

In between the changes at work Sharon and I finally married in August '95. As Asian weddings go this felt more like a gig. Over 800 guests attended which is more than some music bands attract. Food, drink and music were flowing. This was a real party. Live bands were still the norm at Asian weddings and M had provided a good band for £750. This was cheap and to be fair all I could afford at the time. Asian weddings can last for days and most of the time is a whirlwind. You learn to just go with the flow. If someone says smile, you smile; if they say look down, you look down. Quite frankly, you did as you were told. You just wanted the wedding over and done with. My mum and dad did the best they could with the money we had saved. The real financial burden tends to fall on the girl's side and Sharon's side of the family ensured everyone was catered for. The wedding was full of people, colour, music and the odd fallout between relatives, which goes with the territory. As with all Sikh weddings the male has to wear a turban for the religious ceremony. On the day of my wedding my uncles decided to take the responsibility for tying my turban. With no experience or knowledge of tying a turban, they made a complete hash of the situation. Rather than look smart, the turban resembled a speedboat! My mum refused to have my turban retied due to superstition and the marriage failures that ran through our family. She was mindful that everything happened the once. After twenty years I am still reminded of the size of my turban!

Business-wise the next six months proved equally difficult yet we were happy and confident of making the department profitable. Business started to flow through slowly but surely. All the previous hard work was finally coming to fruition. We both had a genuine belief that we would be successful and meet the target set by Mike. Business was good, I was making appointments and converting the sales. What could possibly go wrong?

With 6 months almost up Wendy stated that we had reached the set target and were due a wage rise. At last, I was about to earn some extra cash for all my efforts. A meeting was organised with Mike in the boardroom. The day approached and we had all the documentation and bits of information to support our cause. At the meeting Wendy presented the information and then said can we have a wage rise as agreed. Mike took time to respond and then stated that we had actually missed the target and so no wage rise was due. At this point I was sitting there disappointed; not even a gesture of some sort. It wasn't as though we were even on an average wage. After all that hard work, and then to be told we had not deserved anything was a hard blow to accept. Had we hit the target? I have absolutely no reason to believe we did not. Suddenly Wendy accused Mike of being a liar and going back on his word. Silence was greeted with an air of anticipation. I could see Mike's face turning bright red. Then with a whack on the table, Mike snarled "I am not a liar, how dare you call me a liar!" I had never seen the man like this and, believe me, never wanted to again.

Wendy and I were told to leave and we drove around in her car for a while, contemplating what will happen next. Wendy was in a state of shock at what had just occurred in the meeting with Mike. Within a few days Wendy left the club and suddenly the department was exposed and wide open with a so-called junior now in temporary charge. Rather than be frightened I had this overwhelming feeling I could turn this around. I had learnt the hard way how to generate business. Surely I could make this work. I had no choice. It had to work.

Over the next few days I put a simple plan together and spoke to Joe Elliott, an influential friend of Mark Jones, the Commercial Director, who was left with the task of overlooking the non-match day activities. Quite frankly this was another area he could really do without. The first thing he said to me was to start looking for another job and actually gave me a couple of contacts to call. For some reason the more he said it would not work, the more I became certain it would and I would prove everyone wrong. But I needed a chance, just one chance.

I held a meeting with Mark and Joe and explained that I would make it work within four months. Mark was very reluctant and kept telling me why it would be a waste of mine and the club's time to sell a dead horse. Well this horse is alive and well. Fortuitously I met Mike along the famous sky blue corridors at Highfield Road. It was a chance meeting or an omen and he asked how I was doing. Well this was my chance and I took it and asked to see him for a few minutes. He obliged and I explained that I will turn the business around. What made me think I could do it? When you have nothing in life other than pride you have nothing to lose – I asked for one chance with no wage rise or any other benefit, this was for me. This was a challenge I was going to win. Incredibly Mike agreed, probably because he could see I was genuine and I would do whatever it takes to make this business work. Mark was disappointed, but had no choice and quite frankly gave me no support other than to check his contacts for alternative employment for me.

The first task was to meet all the clients and suppliers of the club and explain that we actually had a Conference Centre. I contacted the local media and explained that Coventry City Football Club now has a Business Centre for all conference and sales needs. It had a professional touch and for me this was my business. I treated the situation as if I was working for myself and Coventry City happened to be one of my clients. I visited many football clubs who operated a conference centre and there were only a select few who had tapped into the non-match day business. I would look for the good ideas and then replicate them. Twice a week I would visit hotels to write down the companies using their facilities and started taking the business to Coventry City with a guarantee of a tour of the ground and opportunity to meet the players. Remember this was a time when we started to purchase several top players like Richard Shaw, John Salako, Robbie Keane and Dion Dublin. Hotels could not compete with this. I looked at all our benefits and homed in on these. I was working all the hours god gave me. This was my business and I was going to make it successful. Most businesses take two years to show some sort of return; I had four months! What did surprise me was the number of football clubs failing to utilise their facilities at the time. They were just working to match days only. It just didn't occur to them that football clubs would be a far more attractive proposition for companies to host their meetings than hotels. Firstly there was no issue with car parking. The venue was interesting; during lunch you could view the dressing rooms or meet some of the players. I took full advantage and very quickly Coventry City F.C. became a destination for companies to host their meetings and conferences.

Within four months we were literally booming. We had won a number of high profile contracts from

Coventry Building Society and Rolls Royce, amongst many others. Each time someone booked they were featured on the web with a testimonial. I started to get more features than the commercial department. I was relentless, I was on a mission. I believed, I had a major desire to make this work and, most importantly, I had the persistence to keep going. Defeat is not in my dictionary; not this time around. I was determined to make this work; in reality I had no choice. On the way I was learning valuable lessons in life and work. I have always been told there are different types of people in this world. Some will help you but want something back in return. Others will help and not expect anything back and believe their good fortune or karma will be returned in another way. They genuinely want to see you do well.

Around this time I met Noel Hand, a big City fan who is now a very close friend of mine. He had various businesses, but one particular business he had interested me. He would coach sales people how to engage with potential customers and subsequently win their business. As someone who always wants to learn, and is fascinated with human behaviour, we became good friends. He would pass on tips to me and always be available to talk. In short he was a positive, motivated person and in life I have tried to surround myself with these types of people. My philosophy is simple. You have one life so why surround yourself with negative people who enjoy other people's misery or problems. Negativity breeds anger, doubt, indecision, all evil pillars of life we can do without. Noel, on the other hand, would always be positive and helped me secure a big contract. Rolls Royce was looking to host a big conference which included many of their senior dignitaries. I spoke to Noel and explained the significance of Coventry City winning this business, as it would send a message to all the other companies that we were a viable destination. After a few coaching tips from Noel I was ready for the meeting. The actual meeting itself went very well and we ticked all the boxes. On leaving, I remember shaking hands with the decision makers and offering them the best for wherever they chose. They had a couple more venues to visit so the waiting game was on. After a few days I received a call to say Coventry City had won the business. On enquiry, which I do with all companies as you can always learn something new, they mentioned it was our approach that won them over. This bugged me for a while, as that was too vague. During the week-long conference I spoke to the organiser who said it was our honesty and humility that did the trick. Some of the others had used the tactic of criticising competing venues. We had actually stated how good all the other venues were and wished them well wherever they decided to go. This resonated with the host and felt we would go the extra mile. Psychologically we had won them over by praising our competitors.

Suddenly Coventry City was a fashionable place to host meetings. Naturally I ensured we received as much PR as possible. We began recruiting for more staff to deal with the explosion of companies contacting us. We had taken on the established venues and beaten them at their own game. I did perhaps take it too far in my quest to be the best venue. I was so engrossed in generating as much money and PR for Coventry City that I could end up doing the most cringeworthy PR stunts. In one particular case I convinced Gordon Strachan and Robbie Keane to have a photograph with me holding up our conference brochures. This made the papers and all the event magazines. In truth they made the publications because of Gordon and Robbie having a starring role. Great PR for Coventry City and the business, but the three of us standing there holding up brochures and smiling as if we were really interested looked dire. I was used to it but I ended up bringing Robbie and Gordon down to my standards.

The football club at the time had an excellent relationship with the Coventry Telegraph. People such as Adam Dent and Andy Turner would support us as much as possible. During testing times in the Championship, I came up with the idea of having John Sillett replicate Lord Kitchener by pointing the finger and having the statement "your club needs you" in big letters. The Telegraph ran the caption on several occasions. Another dodgy PR stunt but it worked. In my books any kind of PR is good. Looking back it was great having the support of John Sillett, but in the background are my colleagues and I smiling away. It wasn't one of my best ideas. Understanding how the media works, I would submit as much information to the Telegraph as possible. The more players in the photos the better, as our press release had every opportunity of being published and for free. At one point we were rivalling Joe Elliott for media space – now that was hard work. I believe we calmed down and took time out when Andy commented that our commercial editorial was being featured more than the club's information, which is what the fans want to read. He had a point. There were times when former players returning to Highfield Road would be persuaded to just have photographs with the commercial staff, which would then be published through the media outlets. Everyone would just look at me and think now what's he up to. During the week I would send the picture to Andy with an editorial and a rent a quote from the player. It never failed to make the papers. I was learning so much about business and didn't even realise it at the time.

After four months Mike called me into his office. He took his time staring at the figures and pondering over my work for the last four months. He appeared to be in profound thought; it felt like a lifetime. What was he thinking? Surely I had kept my side of the bargain, what else could go wrong now? Mind you, in the life of Raj Athwal, nothing is ever simple. Finally he looked up at me and said for the first time we had made a profit and I was to be rewarded. He gave me a wage rise which I fully deserved. I had worked my bollocks off for months. The poignant moment came when the board could not have a meeting due to all the rooms being booked out. Mike had this ability to praise you without really praising you. Hard to explain, but those who knew Mike well will understand. Even Mark Jones started to change his ways towards me and even took some of the credit for the success of the department. That was fine by me. Suddenly I had credibility and Bryan Richardson took no time to let people know he hired me. I was buzzing; things were looking up. Mark wanted me to work in the commercial department, which was a promotion in some ways. But I had built the conference centre and did not want to let go. This was my baby.

This was one of the first harsh business lessons I had learned. Know when it's time to quit and don't embrace the comfort zone. Another harsh lesson learnt was to let go of the fact that I supported Coventry City. The problem was I began sacrificing any commission owed to me each year and only took a basic salary. In my mind I was doing my bit by putting my commission back into the club and just living off a basic wage. This went on until Paul Fletcher arrived and rightly told me I was working for my future and family. He was absolutely right. For a number of years I am sure the commission would have amounted to thousands of pounds and, while many reading this are probably thinking what an idiot, well let me tell you my wife called me words that I could not even find in the Oxford Dictionary. I was not naïve, I actually felt that I was doing a good deed on behalf of the club that gave me my chance in life. However, and as I have learnt to my cost, if you work hard you deserve your reward. What Paul Fletcher said to me was so true. You owe it to your family – work to live, not the other way around. To think if we had Paul at Coventry years before leaving Highfield Road I am sure we would not be in the predicament the club finds itself in now and I would be thousands of pounds better off!

As time went on Mark started to pressure me to join the commercial department and, after three very successful years building up the conference business from a loss to a very profitable organisation, I was content. More importantly, I proved to myself that I could do whatever I wanted. The choice was mine. The club hired a new venue Sales Manager to take over the reins whilst I transferred to the commercial department. I had very little time to work with Mark as he duly left.

During this period I began to liaise with some of the first team players. Commercially, Coventry City was ahead of its time. We were on par with many of the Premiership clubs of today. The club had a reputation for being entrepreneurial and Jimmy Hill played a big part in this. Going to the training ground helped me to get to know the players better. Some of the injured ones would be helpful on match days by meeting some of our corporate customers and I would call in the favours as and when I needed to. Many people outside of the game do complain about players and how players could do more on a match day. While to a point I agree we also need to understand they too are humans and while many feel comfortable playing in front of thousands on a weekly basis, not all have the confidence to speak to two people. What we forget is that they are not robots, and while we watch them on TV and have certain expectations, not all the players were confident speaking to the general public. I know of some Coventry players who would do all they could to avoid being interviewed in the lounges on match days. Lisa Tanner and I would be running all over the place at Highfield Road trying to locate some of the squad players. When we found them they would make all sorts of excuses; you could just tell they were really out of their comfort zone.

On the flip side players such as Noel Whelan, Dion Dublin, Steve Froggatt, Richard Shaw, John Salako, Gary McAllister, Gary McSheffrey, Mustapha Hadji and Chris Kirkland were model professionals. They had their moments but on the whole they were great to work with. The layout of Highfield Road also made it easier to engage with the players. Looking back the corporate facilities at Highfield Road were excellent and had much more of an atmosphere than the Ricoh Stadium. All the guests in the Main Stand were close to the dressing rooms. In the Carling Club, as it was called, the guests had prime views of the away team arriving. Most could simply walk out of their lounge to meet the away players. To think of the calibre of away players we had visiting Highfield Road, we took all this for granted.

With the inception of the Sky deal you could see the Premier League turning into something of a monster. However, during the 90s there was still a balance with the players and security was tight but not at the levels you see now. You could speak to the players as they made their way to the Players' Lounge, signing autographs for the kids. We had a reputation of being a family club and for all home games we would take some of the kids and let them wait near the entrance to where the players arrived. At the side of the Main Stand, where the coach would drop the players off, there was a side entrance for the away team. This is the area many of the kids would be lined up and we never had a complaint from the away team.

On one occasion, when the Manchester United team which won the Champions' League arrived, the kids were excitedly lined up against the wall. These were the mother of all autographs. Even some of the adults tried to fake their way in by claiming the autographs were for their kids. Yeah right, suddenly they had shirts and balls to sign! What I do remember is as the United team arrived not all of their players signed the autographs and some just signed sporadically. The one player who signed every child's autograph book and was the last one in the dressing room was David Beckham. After that day I would refuse to hear anything said against him. When someone of his status takes the time to speak to kids and have photographs before a game you cannot but stop and admire the guy. He is under the same pressure as every other player, but it's as if he understood where he once came from and the fact he is in a privileged position. It doesn't surprise me how he has built a fantastic brand for himself and good luck to him.

Another legendary part of the United set up was Alex Ferguson, a gentleman who always made the time to talk to the Coventry staff. Sir Alex has also gone on record to say Highfield Road was one of his favourite grounds. Probably because two sides of the ground were always full of United fans. On one occasion, I had the privilege of finding him black marker pens for the flipchart in the away dressing room. I happened to be walking by the dressing room area when I heard a broad Glaswegian accent summoning me over to him. He simply said "Son, I need some black marker pens." No problem, leave that with me. Off I went looking everywhere for these black marker pens. Looking back I was actually assisting the opposition, but this was Sir Alex Ferguson. Somehow I got hold of the pens and ran back to the away dressing room. I knocked on the door and just walked in. Sir Alex, who was talking to Eric Cantona, acknowledged me as if to say I will be with you in a few seconds. Now I had time to think, my mind started racing. I am in the Man United dressing room with all the greats. Should I make conversation with one of the players? What would I say? To be honest I was standing there like a lemon staring at the likes of Beckham, Giggs and all the other players while they were stark bollock naked. What made it even more awkward was when one of the players walked up to me and said who are you? "I'm Raj Athwal," I said without thinking. He just stared at me for a second with his bits hanging out as if to say who the fuck is Raj Athwal. He was looking at me inquisitively, probably thinking is this our new club doctor? What with my academic record, I don't think so. He gave the impression he was excited and up for the game! Luckily by this time Sir Alex came over to where I was standing and thanked me for the pens before telling me to do one. Just as I left Gordon Strachan clocked me and started questioning what I was doing in the Man United dressing room. As a joke, I said I was discussing the Coventry team line up. Gordon wasn't amused and I had to explain that I was just delivering some pens. To be honest I am not sure to this day whether he did believe me or not. To make matters worse we lost the game 2-1 with John Aloisi scoring for us. Let's just say I kept out of Gordon's way for a while.

Gordon Strachan was a great guy to have around. He had this persona and presence about him. Some people have this ability to be noticed as soon as they walk into a room. When he spoke people listened. For Coventry City he was a coup and part of Bryan Richardson's vision for the club. We all genuinely believed that with Gordon at the helm Coventry was on the verge of something big. By this I mean Europe. With the players we were prepared to invest in surely sooner or later lady luck would take us to new heights. Looking back we had assembled a quality side that could beat anyone on our day. Players such as Dion Dublin, John Salako, Magnus Hedman, Gary McAllister, Robbie Keane, Hadji, Roland

Nilsson, Darren Huckerby and Noel Whelan had something about them. They were all quality performers. Gordon could do no wrong. For a couple of seasons we played some of the best football we had seen since the days of John Sillett and George Curtis. One season we were even labelled the entertainers. There was a swagger about the team. It was young and fearless. Life is about opportunities and taking chances. We had our opportunity and we had the chance to progress.

While Gordon had lost players of the calibre of Dion Dublin, George Boateng and Darren Huckerby, I do believe the departures of Gary McAllister and Robbie Keane a season later came back to haunt us and eventually see the club relegated from the top league for the first time in its history. They were our two top goal scorers and would be hard to replace. I remember the day a key player was sold, allegedly without Gordon's say so. I was at the training ground that day and Gordon just looked at me and said that he didn't want him to go. He had received a call from Bryan saying an offer had been accepted. Gordon didn't apparently have a say. So much was out of his control. The club had to survive on limited resources, yet we were playing with fire by trying to punch too far above our weight. When Gary McAllister and Robbie Keane moved on you could feel the despair at the club. Even though we were in the Premiership, for the first time as an employee and a fan I felt something was wrong. The Coventry City I knew and was working for was changing. It was like being aboard the coach in the film Speed. The club appeared to be running out of control and we all didn't know where it would end. At every management meeting, we would all be under pressure to bring in more revenue. The sales team were working flat out. We had achieved what we set out to do and more. The pressure from the top became relentless; it was evident we were living on borrowed time. As a sales team we were victims of our own success. We were almost sold out and overachieving in most areas. Rather than congratulate us, the perception was we could do more. In theory that's true. What many accountants fail to understand is to do more you need more resources, training and a productive, positive environment.

Not everyone can succeed in the football sales environment. The products we are selling change week to week. To be successful there is a need to build long-term relationships. Most clubs work on short-term gain and that will never work. During my time in football I have disproved the misconceptions that off pitch activities in football are largely reliant on what goes on over 90 minutes on the pitch. By challenging the mindsets at the clubs I have worked for we reached unprecedented levels of commercial success. During difficult periods you can always find an amusing distraction.

During this particular episode it involved Gordon Strachan. Most clubs tend to have a players' kit sponsorship featured in the match day programme. Businesses and supporters can put their name next to their favourite player and have it appear in each match day programme. Gordon happened to have a secondary sponsor with Electronix, a local electrical shop and a relative of mine. They say never mix pleasure with relatives; well I decided to go against the grain and take some money off my cousin Colin Bahia. Colin, to be fair, was always on hand to support the club any way he could. On this occasion he mentioned that as part of his sponsorship he was happy to offer Gordon any deal on electrical goods in his store. A deal normally means a good discount in my books. Dealing with Gordon I should have known better and not left the word deal open to interpretation. When I mentioned this to Gordon he perked up and said he just so happened to be after one of these huge LED TVs. I gave Gordon the details and thought nothing of it. That was until I received a call from Colin a few weeks later ranting and raving down the phone to me. Gordon had apparently walked into the store, ordered the TV and walked out without paying. Colin thought nothing of it and expected Gordon to pay in due course. Weeks later still no payment and, to make matters worse, Colin had even given Gordon a free expensive cabinet for good measure. Colin threatened to take the TV back and Gordon eventually paid up. I asked Colin whether he had given Gordon a discount. He literally made nothing from the TV and threw in a complimentary cabinet as part of the service.

Days later at a reserve team game Gordon stopped me, looked me straight in the eyes and said I never got a discount. When I explained Colin had given him the TV at cost price Gordon wouldn't budge. Gordon had interpreted the discount to be free! Never again did I ever accept a discount offer for players. I had to laugh when Colin phoned me again a few weeks later. Gordon was now using the free retailer's car park in Coventry city centre behind Colin's store to park his car and then walk thorough Colin's shop to do his shopping. When he finished he simply walked back through the shop and exited via the staff room without a word to anyone. Colin was too shocked to stop him and allowed him to carry on. I had to take my hat off to Gordon; the man was a genius.

On another occasion Bryan Richardson had arranged to play the mighty Bayern Munich in a friendly at Highfield Road. This was mid-season, 27th January 1998 to be precise. Although we lost the game 4-2 the only real memory I have of the evening is asking the Bayern and German World Cup winning captain Lothar Matthaus for one of the players' shirts after the match. He was very approachable and I thought I would try my luck.

This was Bayern Munich, after all. Lothar beckoned me into the away dressing room. Unfortunately all the shirts were swapped with the Coventry players and just as I was about to leave the dressing room, disappointed, Lothar stopped me. Christian Nerlinger, who played that night, still had his shirt with him. Without any hesitation Lothar walked over and after a brief discussion, Christian handed his shirt over to me. After thanking and wishing them both well for the remainder of the season I left to go home. The shirt was going to take pride in my house. When I arrived home that evening I placed the dirty drenched sweaty shirt on one of the chairs to dry. The idea was to have the shirt framed and placed on my living room wall. Unbeknown to me the next morning Sharon, seeing the state of the shirt, put it straight into the washing machine on high temperature. My face was a picture when the shirt came out of the machine. It had shrunk so much it would look tight on a five-year-old. I was gobsmacked. To make matters worse Sharon told me not to bring dirty sweaty second hand shirts home again as they were hard to wash! To add further insult to injury, the next day Mark Jones asked me to bring the shirt in for Gordon Strachan. I had only opened my big mouth about the shirt and Gordon, finding out, wanted to give it to his son Gavin. You can imagine the look when I brought this extra small sized shirt in to the club. Incredibly, nothing was ever said, though I learned my lesson to never leave any football memorabilia near my wife and keep my mouth shut!

The club eventually appointed a new Commercial Director called Rik Allison. An ex RAF man, we all feared the worst. How wrong we could be! This was a true gentleman, a man of integrity, fairness and always backed his team no matter what the situation. It was a pleasure to serve under Rik. Interestingly Rik had no commercial experience in football but charmed the pants off the board. I remember Mike telling me why he chose Rik – he was the only one of the candidates interviewed to accept a glass of whiskey at the actual interview and that was good enough for Mike. For now things could not have been better. My first child, Simran, was born, I had just bought my own house and I had secured another pay rise. Just for the record and after four to five years at the club I was still on a poor salary as a Sales Manager. We were surviving and I was planning for my future. All good things come to those who wait, I kept getting told. If money is the be all and end all then you will not learn a single thing in business. It takes time and fortunes will eventually appear. Learning and networking with the best businesspeople is worth as much in value in the early days as earning a good income later on in life. You have to build blocks as you go on in life or career. Miss out particular blocks and they may come back to haunt you. It's no different to studying for your GCSEs and then jumping straight onto a degree. It is important to build the foundations before you progress and progress you will if you want to – it's your choice. Challenge yourself to stretch the boundaries.

Under the stewardship of Rik I was really enjoying my time at Coventry; the club was progressing well in the Premiership and business off the pitch was booming. In a way it is so easy to become order takers in the Premiership. Most games are sponsored and companies that would not give you the time of day phone you literally pleading to become a sponsor for one of the big fixtures. For some inherent reason I have always had the ability to motivate myself and push the boundaries. This comes from being competitive at what I am good at and knowing how hard I had to work during my school and University years. I want to be the best. This was the same at Coventry City FC. I loved my job and bringing new clients on board gave me a buzz. We were selling out and suddenly I was looking for new ideas to generate further revenue. This was important to keep me challenged and essentially to keep raising the stakes. Some people I have worked with in football are content with just doing what they need to. That's fine by me, as long as they are doing what's expected of them. However, the issue arises when they complain about being overlooked for promotion, or failed to negotiate a wage rise. What I have learnt over the years is if you put in the effort somewhere down the line you will get your rewards. Reap what you sow.

There was such a camaraderie at the club, it really was like a family. George Curtis would always be around, helping out at the Mercers Arms pub opposite the ground and the pools office. Micky Gynn would pop in every so often on his post round. This I found difficult to deal with at first. Micky Gynn was one of my heroes back in the 80s. I just didn't realise at the time that they were on good wages, but not good enough to retire on. Barry Powell and Ray Gooding also worked at the club in various capacities. The club's policy was simple; where possible employ from within. It felt as if almost every other person was related to someone at the club. This clearly was not the case but the point is it was a close knit club; everyone looked after each other.

Pre-season was always interesting, as this is when the real commercial work is completed. To this day I still get asked what I do during the summer and whether I take three months off on holiday. Anybody working in the commercial departments of football clubs will tell you from June onwards it is relentless. You have huge budgets to achieve based on selling seasonal memberships, executive boxes, advertising boards, player sponsorship and any other partnership revenue streams you may have. The bulk part of the commercial revenue is generated during pre-season. To any outsider this may sound strange. However this is the case, while the remainder of the season is utilised to fill in the sponsorship gaps, nurture potential clients and ensure the existing customers are content. From October I would start planning for the season after and have a timeline of projects that need completing. Budgets are then based on your projections and begin from December onwards. The final draft for budgets varies, though I found at Coventry we had to submit these in January and have them fully approved by the board by March.

During the majority of seasons we would be asked to submit two sets of projections; one for the Premiership and one for the Championship. Most, if not all, clubs hovering near relegation do the same. It's just being prudent if the worst was to happen. During the remainder of the season I had a time management plan which I would discuss with the commercial team. The Sales Executives at the time were excellent and just knew what was required from them. As a department we were strong and everyone knew their role. Much of this was also down to the excellent leadership of Rik Allison. Employees such as Julie Grimmett, Lisa Tanner and Clive Weare would leave nothing to chance and were an absolute pleasure to work with. During this period I also became close friends with Paul Coles, who was Head of Retail. His business acumen was second to none and I learned so much from the way he managed his department. While his tenure at Coventry City was short, it's no surprise he is now a well respected and successful business consultant in New Zealand. On the conference side we had employed Hermione Heavey, another Coventry person who was very talented at her job. Hermione and I became good friends and I was delighted to be invited to her engagement party. That was until I realised the party was being held at a notorious pub in the middle of Bell Green. I shit myself and made my excuses. Well, the truth is out, sorry Hermione.

During the Championship years there appeared to be a merry go round of employees, especially in the commercial department. Much of this I believe was down to the pressures of generating revenue in the Championship. However, we employed some gems who could hold their own in this league. People such as Suzette Johnson, Natalie Stevens, Caroline Lissaman and Alan Falconbridge were excellent members of the commercial team, though Alan was a typical lad's lad and I would have to be on his case constantly. Alan was a great kid, honest and loyal and always ready to help anyone. Alan constantly tested my patience but was always prepared to go the extra mile when required.

I still remember the day Geoffrey Robinson, Chairman and former paymaster general during the Tony Blair government, allegedly decided to take away my managerial status without any consultation with me. This was during the time when Paul Fletcher was appointed CEO. A meeting was held with the club Directors. Almost immediately after the meeting a memo was sent to all the club employees of the changes that were proposed. One of the changes was to strip me of my Commercial Manager's status. I only discovered this after reading the memo. There was no meeting, no HR involved, in fact it was so blasé I thought it was a mistake. Ken Sharp, the Commercial Director, confirmed my fears and said Geoffrey had made the decision. I'm not sure to this day how or why the decision was made. However, what has always made me smile is Alan Falconbridge walking into my office immediately after reading the memo committing his loyalty to me. That was priceless and typified Alan. For days I was pissed off and could not understand why Geoffrey did what he did. To add insult to injury, he then wanted me to go canvassing with him, knocking on the doors of householders in Holbrooks seeking their vote in the upcoming elections. I duly did this and ensured I gave a good account for the Conservative Party as opposed to Labour! In all fairness to Paul Fletcher he did not make the change, as he realised this would have a negative impact on both myself and the department. Now that's called man management.

From the middle of August onwards we would be flat out trying to fill the gaps. We would also be visiting existing customers and sourcing new companies or businesses which were looking to re-locate to the area. Most Chambers of Commerce have an Inward Investment team. After liaising with them, it was agreed that we would offer an executive box for selected matches if they were hosting new companies in the area. This would give me first call on meeting the Directors without having to go through all the normal sales routes. The only problem was the Inward Investment team did not want to entertain potential multi-million pound businesses on a Saturday afternoon, as it was their weekend off. These are companies interested in moving to the Coventry & Warwickshire area which would potentially generate hundreds, if not thousands, of jobs.

My suggestion of our sales team entertaining the new companies didn't go down well either. Sometimes you have to make the sacrifices.

Aside from football, we would also have a calendar of events such as the annual golf day, sporting dinners and the end of season awards dinner. The golf day would be a guaranteed sell out. What I have noticed over the years is a gradual change in players' interests and hobbies. From 2000 onwards there has been a marked decrease in the number of players taking up golf. Towards the end of my time at Coventry and my whole time at Watford only the older players could play the game of golf. The younger ones had no interest in the sport and games consoles began taking over. I am sure it's only a matter of time before the golf day is replaced by a Football Manager day whereby customers pay to play players on consoles!

Sporting dinners, which were popular until the 2000s, has also seen a decline in attendances. Guests are looking for something different and you have to be thinking outside the box to generate any interest. The football industry is no different to any other and you have to continually be evolving and continue to learn and change. During the 1990s hospitality and memberships dominated off the pitch. The 2000s witnessed a move to networking and partnerships. Recent times have seen the bigger clubs globalise their activities worldwide. This is an idea I spoke to Joe Elliott about way back in the late 1990s. I felt as a club we had the opportunity to begin contacting global companies to forge partnerships and more importantly generate revenue. While Joe was on board the idea never really materialised, with Coventry City having to contend with other more pressing issues on and off the pitch.

What I did notice was the inception of end of season award dinners at large venues with no expense spared. Coventry City Football Club had been way ahead of the game by hosting the Coventry City Ball since the 60s and 70s. After a hiatus Rik and I brought the awards dinner back, but in a bigger and more modern way. The players all looked forward to the event, which speaks volumes of the organisers. Even during my time at Rangers I noticed many of the events were not being as well attended as previously. It appears football on and off the pitch was going through a transitional period, and many who worked in the game needed to stop thinking the conventional way and become more creative and entrepreneurial.

If there was an annual event at Coventry we all looked forward to, it was the staff Christmas parties held at Highfield Road. Wendy and I organised the first one during the 1995/96 season, which was tame compared to the later ones. The Christmas parties were well attended and it was an opportunity for all the staff to get to know one another. Parties are great, but they can also bring out the worst in people. One year I was hosting the party with my colleagues John Street and Lesley Brooks. As John worked in finance we made certain of making this a great party for all to enjoy. As was custom at club parties, drinks and food was always paid for by the board. We would all do our best to thank them for such generosity by drinking the place dry. The Board of Directors and the management team from Ryton training ground would all attend. The only staff not invited would be the players. Not sure why, but they were kept apart from the non-playing staff, which I found strange bearing in mind we all worked for the same organisation. During one particular Christmas party, and while everyone was in full swing, I allegedly got hold of the microphone from the DJ and allegedly started calling Bryan Richardson a wanker. Unlike previous seasons, when the speakers would be crackly, these were clear as daylight. To make matters worse the speakers were positioned throughout the Premier Club so even the hard of hearing could not complain. I would have stopped but people started cheering and giving me the thumbs up as if to offer me their approval to carry on; and that was just the members of the board! They must have misunderstood me, thinking I was calling him a banker! John got hold of the microphone before I said too much, but the damage was done.

The next day, knowing full well what had occurred the night before, I decided to keep a low profile. That didn't last long as I walked through Thackhall Street reception. There was a warm welcome from many of my colleagues packed into the small reception area. The talk was all about what I had called the Club Chairman the night before. To say I was sheepish is an understatement. It was completely out of character.

Later that morning, I received a call from Lesley, Bryan's PA. Bryan Richardson wanted to see me. That was it; career over before it had even started. As I made my way to see Bryan I was making up more excuses than the political parties put together. In all honesty I couldn't think straight; I was in deep shit. Once I arrived at his office, which took no more than a minute, he summoned me to sit down. Bryan had this strict headmaster type of persona which only made matters worse for me. He also has a habit of making you wait before he starts speaking. I have seen people in authority do this often and am not sure if this is to make people nervous or feel inferior. It must be a psychological approach to make them feel in a position of power. Well, it had worked with me. In this case he was intensely reading some paperwork, probably taking in how much money the club owed its creditors. It really did feel like a court case and I was guilty as hell. I had no defence and he had the authority to do whatever he wanted. It must be noted Coventry City never officially had an HR department. Bryan was the HR department. After a few seconds, which felt like a lifetime, he looked up at me, smiled and said what did you think about last night? I started mumbling an apology and all the excuses I could think of, such as how I still get confused with certain English swear words, how my wife would divorce me without this job and all that sort of nonsense. He stopped me mid-conversation and said it was a great night and well done for organising the party, and to keep to the same format next year. I just stared at him, waiting for the poignant question of, what exactly did you refer to me as last night? It never came and he just stared at me as if to say off you go, young man, do some work; make some money and plenty of it as the club has a huge debt to service.

Walking out of his door, I was bemused and relieved at the same time. The emotions were in full flow from one extreme to the other. Had I really got away with calling the Chairman something unsavoury? To make matters worse I really could not remember what I had actually said and was only going on hearsay from 100 witnesses! Never again, lesson learnt; my motto is to stick to tomato juice in future.

In 2000/01 we had a tough season on the pitch, which resulted in the club becoming relegated for the first time from the top league. This was a shock to the staff, players, management and supporters. For the first time in 34 years Coventry City F.C. had just got relegated. This was unheard of and, no matter what position the club would be in the table, there was always an instinctive feeling we would get out of any difficult position – not in this instance. We were down and out. Within two seasons we had lost players of the calibre of Dion Dublin, Gary McAllister, Robbie Keane and were clearly short of quality goalscorers. Craig Bellamy arrived as the saviour but he was recovering from an injury and by his own admission did not perform to the best of his ability. Since leaving Coventry we have seen Craig set the Premiership alight for other clubs. The timing was just wrong for both club and player. The Premiership was becoming more and more competitive and we needed quality. Inside the club there was a general feeling that we would survive another season in the Premiership and continue building the squad thereafter. After the first three games, which we had won two and lost one, there was a positive mood inside the club. While we didn't expect to set the league on fire, there was an expectation in the club that we would finish in a respectable mid-table position. Relegation was not on the agenda.

Even though the Premiership was attracting some of the best players in the world, the question of attendances always cropped up in management meetings. For a population of over 350,000 we rarely reached capacity. Our average crowds bordered on 20,000 and commercially I know this had an impact on how strong we were financially. The club was paying way over the top in wages. This was unsustainable, even with the Premiership money. The shirt sponsorship fee helped but was nowhere near the figures an average Premiership club can attract in today's market. The club was in a difficult predicament with finances. Getting the pricing policy just right is difficult, especially when you are under pressure to generate more revenue. In reality there are no right or wrong answers. Football is a fluid industry and a winning team will always attract supporters.

During the season there was some respite when we signed John Hartson. From February to early April we had only lost two matches in eight. I remember speaking to club secretary Graham Hover at this time. He was absolutely positive we would survive relegation. He had seen many relegation dog fights and the omens looked good during this period. Going into the last four matches we knew we had to win as many as possible. Statistics will show we had to win all four to stay up. After beating Sunderland 1-0 at home everyone at the club really thought we would survive against all the odds. Unfortunately we lost three and drew against Bradford, scoring two in the process. For the record, and in my opinion, the Liverpool result sent us down. Even if we had beaten Aston Villa and Bradford, with the results going against us, we would have been relegated. We were also the second lowest goalscorers after Bradford. It's so easy to criticise and we can all become managers, but the writing was on the wall when our two key players left the previous summer and had not been adequately replaced. I still believe if Gordon was allowed to keep the players he wanted, we would still have been in the Premiership that season.

Looking back, we were on the precipice of something special, we just fell short and are now paying for poor decision making. Gordon mentioned he believed he had stayed two years too long. We can all fall into the comfort zone trap and Gordon was no different. You try and kid yourself that you need another year before moving on. That year never happens. The real challenge is to make a decision, give yourself a real timeline and work to it. I too am a victim of the comfort zone situation. It gets a hold of the person; life is too easy. You think there is another challenge but the challenge died years ago. New personnel arrive and you end up challenging them for bringing in new ideas. That's the time to wave goodbye to your comfort zone.

One of my personal highlights during the relegation season was arranging for the Two Tone Collective to play at Highfield Road prior to the Southampton match in December. As was normal practice in management meetings, the question of attendances cropped up. The Southampton fixture was an evening match and suggestions were welcomed to increase the attendance. It's difficult to offer solutions as to what can increase attendances other than a winning team. Any extra activity on the pitch for me is merely added value. Supporters do not pay good money just to watch pre-match entertainment, that's an extra not the main event. I had been to watch a play about Ska music at the Belgrade Theatre and was fortunate to meet Pauline Black and Ranking Roger at the after show. I suggested to Ranking Roger that it would be great to get their new 2 Tone Collective band playing at Highfield Road, as the city is home to Ska music. From a brief conversation at the Belgrade Theatre things developed very quickly as I convinced the board that this was something different and had not been done before. If nothing else, the music would be enjoyed by most of the supporters and Ska music was making a mini revival at the time.

My main dealing was with Roger Lomas, who was managing the band. Roger was responsible for producing the Special's first single "Gangsters" at his home in Broad Street, Coventry. There appeared to be a stumbling point as the Two Tone Collective were booked to play outside the Cathedral a week after the Southampton match. The problem here was playing at Highfield Road a week earlier took away the nostalgia and the selling point of performing at the Cathedral first. We could not change the dates as it coincided with other events. Roger was keen to cash in on both events, but the city centre management team understandably were not sure. In the end the band were allowed to play the gig at Highfield Road a week earlier to ensure the band members didn't lose out on their pay day. Music, like football, is fluid and they had to cash in while they were popular. This became a personal event for me as I had sold this to the board and, as far as they were concerned, we were expected to sell a few thousand more seats as a result. The only drawback was the gig was in two weeks' time. There had been a delay due to the event organisers for the city centre gig not being comfortable with the Two Tone Collective playing a week earlier. Eventually, along with Steven, a work experience lad working at Coventry at the time, we organised everything from poster designs to actually fly posting with local firms in the area. With previous knowledge of fly posting, Steven and I ensured that the event was very well publicised, albeit we only had two weeks to do so. We then had a problem with the posters. Each time they were advertised enthusiasts would steal them. They were unique and well designed with a large picture of the Jacobean and became a collector's item. Each day Steve and I would make the rounds to the different poster sites in Coventry. In most of the cases the posters were stolen and needed replacing. This was also becoming expensive and time consuming. What frustrated me most were posters of popular chart bands still on the walls and our posters would be stolen within 24 hours. It was not even a case of sabotage, as the posters were cleanly taken off the walls. There was only so much we could fund so we advertised in all other publications, including the match day programme. The event was on a cold Friday night in December. We had converted part of the kiosk area in the Sky Blue Stand into a dressing room and dining area for the band and their guests. A large stage had been erected between the away and home supporters. At the time the band took to the stage, I remember there were over 3,000 people in the ground. To have so many supporters in the ground over an hour before kick-off is unheard of at most football grounds. They played most of the hits from the Specials, Selector and The Beat. It was a unique evening made even more special watching the players and management teams of both Coventry and Southampton dancing away to the music. Security had raised a concern about the away supporters, but this was music, a universal language, and the Southampton fans enjoyed the show as much as anyone else in the ground. To me it proved again anything in life is achievable if you focus the mind.

Over pre-season a sense of reality and optimism set in. Surely with the squad we had we would bounce back to the Premiership. In fact this should become one of the greatest seasons as we beat teams for fun. The Premiership was on hold for one season. I remember one strange moment, prior to the Championship kick off, speaking to Bryan Richardson in the Highfield Road toilets of all places. There we are having a piss and me telling Bryan how the Championship would be fantastic as we will win most of our matches and return back to the Premiership. He agreed with such enthusiasm; I could see him turning to talk to me which would have been a disaster. Luckily he stopped at the right moment. In all honesty the damage was done and he was en route to becoming one of the most controversial Chairman ever to take office at Coventry City. We both knew this was a potential disaster and teams would raise their game against us. I genuinely felt most people at the club thought this but dared not say so, including me.

From a business angle the sales team really had to put the work in and, for many, this was out of their comfort zone. Most clients renewed on the basis we would get straight back to the Premiership and so did not want to lose their seats. After the first two years in the Championship sales became harder and some of the staff began to lose their way and many eventually left the club. I had put the work in from day one in the Championship. I ensured all customers were spoken to and pulled in some favours for sponsorships of less appealing matches. Importantly, and in retrospect, the early days of cold calling and acquiring a can do attitude, kept me going and ensured that we continued to keep bringing new customers on board.

We had to be much more creative and push the boundaries. I was not about to throw in the towel after everything we had collectively achieved. You certainly discover the ones that are prepared to give it their all when the tide is against you.

We went from selling the football to now selling the business. This has been my angle since the Championship. It's also important to understand how businesses change over time and transcend the conventional ways of thinking. Most companies are great at conception but cannot see a project through, or even have a vision beyond the foundations. You have to keep reinventing and changing your benefits every two-three years. Have a plan of action and see it through.

In 2001 the ITV digital contract collapsed. Like most clubs, the money was factored in to pay the bills or maintain the debt. Fortunately Subaru, our shirt sponsors, agreed to continue with the shirt sponsorship for another season. Ironically, relegation had a positive impact business wise. There was an air of optimism among the businesses and most membership areas were at Premiership levels. I discovered there is a reverse effect from businesses when facing adversity. Decision makers wanted to support the club even more so and I realised over time people are prepared to give any organisation a couple of years grace if struggling.

The first game in the Championship was away to Stockport. I had arranged the infamous corporate trip to Edgeley Park and, as always, the coach was oversubscribed. It was a great day out with Lee Hughes scoring and the City winning 2-0. It was only the first match of the season, though the thoughts were of how easy this league will be and how the Premiership is on hold for a season. However, the next four games were a virtual disaster with only one point to show. The Grimsby fixture at Highfield Road became the low point with a 1-0 home defeat, and Gordon Strachan looked a broken man. You could sense the fans' frustration and, luckily for Gordon, Andy Harvey, the Kitman, was on hand when a supporter tried to remonstrate with Gordon. That evening Gordon left through the side door and, with the Chairman and Directors staying longer than expected after the game, we knew there were about to be casualties. Days later Gordon was dismissed and Roland Nilsson became player manager.

Roland was a popular player among the fans and an intelligent character off the pitch. His first ten matches in charge took us to the top of the Championship and for once we looked like a formidable squad that would set the pace. During this period Bryan Richardson decided to bring in his good friend Jim Smith as a consultant to assist Roland. While it has never been publicly discussed, Roland was never happy with the arrangement and when Jim became chief coach this irked Roland. In fairness to Roland, he had the squad playing as a team and they were hard to beat. The Jim Smith appointment never worked and an unbeatable team became disjointed and unpredictable. Another one of Bryan Richardson's decisions that was to come back and haunt him very soon.

Behind the scenes there were issues to contend with. We were seriously in the red and needed to offload some of the senior players who were still earning Premiership wages. The reality of the Championship had set in. There was a balancing act of trying to keep a squad good enough to challenge for the league title or, as a minimum, secure a play-off place.

Everything came to a head in January when Bryan Richardson was ousted. I still remember Bryan walking along the corridors at the Thackhall Street offices carrying his cardboard box. As he made his way down the stairs we all heard him shout to his PA and anyone in earshot that he would be back! While I will always be grateful to Bryan for offering me an opportunity, some of his business decisions had a negative impact on the lives of normal working people. I am not suggesting Bryan made these decisions alone, though as a collective it had a detrimental effect on people. Prior to relegation I had never heard of any employee being made redundant. From 2001 onwards it became a serious concern, and making low paid employees redundant is not always the answer.

One of the highlights and respite from the Championship was the home tie against Tottenham in the third round of the F.A. Cup. All the comparisons to 1987 came flooding back and commercially was an opportunity to maximise the revenue. One of the ideas we had was to invite all the 1987 squad alongside George Curtis and John Sillett. John was still a regular at the club and hosted the corporate suites on match days. Fortunately I had all their contact details – I had kept in regular touch with most of the players – so it really was a case of their availability. Once I had called all the players and convinced them to attend the only missing piece of the jigsaw was George Curtis. From the moment I arrived at Coventry City George was always good to me and supported me whenever there was a need. However, I also knew never to get on the wrong side of George as he would have no hesitation of picking you up by the ears for a few seconds that felt more like a lifetime.

I witnessed this first hand when a young lad called Chris joined the commercial department and decided to have a joke with George. Unfortunately, George did not see the funny side and chased Chris around the cars in Thackhall Street. Now George still had pace and on catching Chris picked him up by the ears to teach him a lesson. We all felt Chris's pain so I shudder to think how Chris must have felt. Well, we did know, as we had to shout at Chris for a week before he could hear us properly!

On another occasion, Leigh Jenkinson, a recruit from Hull City, must have annoyed George. Now Leigh was a tall lad but all I saw was George walk over to Leigh and squeeze his ears so hard he squealed. Leigh used his common sense and walked away with burning red ears. The point was very simple: do not mess with George Curtis. Obviously George was just having a laugh but sometimes I don't think George even knew his own strength.

With regards to the F.A. Cup game we had confirmations from all of the players, and I had even tracked down Brian Kilkline, who was in Portugal on

Picture of me aged 3 or 4

Mum & Dad (Ajit Singh & Parkash Kaur)

Me in the middle as a toddler in our back garden

Celebrating my brother Sonny's 3rd birthday

Parkgate Junior School cup final team mates 1981 – From top left to right
(myself, Steven Powell, ?, Paul Hand and Alan Simmonds)

Bally and Me trying to look super cool circa 1987

Night out at University

Enjoying the music on stage at the University Ball

COVENTRY CITY FOOTBALL CLUB LIMITED

BR\lsb

21 December 1994

Sukhraj Athwal

Holbrooks
COVENTRY

Dear Mr Athwal

Thank you for your letter dated 14 December.

Please give my secretary, Lesley Brooks a call, sometime in the
new year, and she will arrange a suitable time for you to come
in and see me.

Yours sincerely

BRYAN RICHARDSON
CHAIRMAN

CCFC letter – A letter from Chairman Bryan
Richardson agreeing to meet me in the New Year –
a career that has spanned over 20 years

The club agree for me to be part of the 1995/96 pre-season team photo -
the catch being I had to be Sky Blue Sam!

Bringing Robbie Keane and Gordon Strachan down to my standards!
Publicising the facilities at Coventry City

The Two Tone Collective in concert at Highfield Road Stadium 2001 which
included Pauline Black (The Selector); Ranking Roger (The Beat) and Roddy
Radiation (The Specials)

In the company of Sky Blue Legends Bill Glazier, Jimmy Hill, Willie Carr, Chris Kirkland and Tommy Hutchison

The 1987 FA Cup winning squad reunion I organised in 2001

My oldest daughter Simran in her Coventry City kit

Coventry City staff team where I managed to persuade Dave Bennett, Micky
Gynn and Trevor Peake to join us – we still lost the game!
(I am seated second from right)

In the Coventry City dressing room at Highfield Road with legends George Curtis and John Sillett – the photographer decided against telling Cyrille Regis to move!

Launching the business alliance at Rangers with Ally McCoist and Derek Bond (Bond Chartered Accountants)

The mother of all trophy rooms at Ibrox Stadium

With the Coventry and Rangers Legend Mark Hateley

Family photo with Simran, Sharon and Ria

Sharon and I in Rome

Celebrating Christmas at our local

Athwal v Athwal

some hippie mission at the time. The task itself was not easy and I had to persuade one or two who either had other prior arrangements or did not feel comfortable with a reunion. On a personal note, this was not just about the Spurs match or generating revenue; they were players I grew up watching and admired. If I could pull off this feat it would make so many people happy and the players could rekindle lost friendships. I was determined to make this work. It became an obsession, in a good way. Eventually all the players confirmed their attendance.

However, one missing link remained – George Curtis. At first George was reluctant to return, as he felt it was the players who should have all the gratitude and he genuinely meant that. However, after much persuasion he agreed on the condition that he did not have to walk out of the tunnel with the players, as it was their day. That sums up the great George Curtis, who never turned me down for any function. Whenever George was required the club would ask me to approach him. George had worked in several departments and when I joined the club was Head of the Pools Office. Sometimes you felt George knew everyone in Coventry. He had been Commercial Manager of Coventry City for many years and had built up solid relationships with some of the bigger firms in the city. He also taught me about relationship marketing and how it's important to stay in touch with customers regularly. It may seem like a no brainer, yet many businesses complain of feeling isolated once they had committed to the club. People buy from people, he would constantly remind me – never forget that. If it was a worthwhile cause I would ask and other times I would leave it to George to decide. I would like to think George knew I had no agenda. I was just a Coventry City fan doing my best for the club.

Coventry City was my life – it meant everything to

me. I was living the dream. To maximise revenue we ordered replica shirts and had the names and numbers of the players printed. Each player was then sponsored by a business. The idea was to have each player sign their respective shirt and then personally hand it over to the customer. The only issue was we had agreed for the shirts to be framed. We pulled out all the stops to get the local framer to wait for the shirts to be signed on the evening, I then drove to the framers, who in turn had to get all the shirts framed and returned before the end of the game. I'm not sure how he did it but we received the shirts on time and no one was any the wiser. That was a close call, although it generated thousands for the club and that's not including the match and match ball sponsorships. How we missed the Premiership!

The squad of '87 were incredibly sociable and certainly different to the perception of the modern day player. Hosted in the aptly named George Curtis Suite, adults and kids were allowed in to meet and talk to the squad. What I did notice was the respect the squad still had for George and John. Fourteen years on and the former players were addressing George and John as Gaffers. That's the respect the two commanded, and also proves the loyalty and spirit of the players. On closer inspection I realised many of the players were still drinking beer in half pint glasses. Keith Houchen explained George Curtis would allow players to drink as long as they were in half pint glasses, so as not to draw attention. Psychologically drinking half a pint was much more acceptable than finding a player drinking a pint. The stories were flowing on the day about how the management team handled players back then. During the away matches if George and John sensed tension in the squad they would stop off at a pub and allow the players a few drinks. The players would soon start opening up and the problem was nipped in the bud. How the modern game has changed. During the famous cup run some of the players mentioned how they would have a shot of brandy to calm the nerves before a game. During the semi-final game against Leeds one of the players, a teetotaller, was given a shot of brandy along with the other players. Having one shot too many, he started singing loudly. The other players joined in and at one point some of the Leeds players were stood listening outside the Coventry dressing room not realising what was going on. I am sure that gave Coventry a psychological edge!

The occasion was also the first time the full squad, including George and John, had gathered together and to the best of my knowledge the last ever time. The process of trying to bring the squad together was no mean feat. In all honesty the revenue was an excuse to bring the legends back to Highfield Road. The club financially could not refuse. To make the event successful, in my opinion, we needed the full squad. Some players did not want to attend for reasons known to them, though this had nothing to do with the club itself, more about personality clashes. Brian Kilkline eventually changed his plans to attend after I repeatedly called him. I actually convinced his good lady, who in turn influenced Brian. We got there in the end.

There was constant talk about redundancies and soon the club decided to part company with Rik, which was unfortunate, as in my opinion there were plenty of other senior staff who should have gone before him. I was Commercial Manager at this point in time and, to be fair to Rik, he had let me get on with the department ever since his appointment. One of his strengths was allowing managers to manage, similar to Mike.

Another sad moment for me and many of the staff was the departures of Roy and Marie, who were responsible for the welfare of the youth kids at Ryton Training Ground. For me they were part of the sky blue furniture and were unsung heroes for all their work, effort and dedication in ensuring all the youths staying at Ryton were cared for. They also had the responsibility of taking care of the training ground facilities. They acted as guardians for the kids and kept the first team squad in check. They had connecting rooms, allowing them direct access to the Ryton facility. Coventry City had an advantage over many other clubs in that having Roy and Marie to look over the kids appealed to parents. These were 16-year-old kids living away from home for the first time and while football was their primary role, there are many other distractions that come with being associated with a football club. Roy was always a step ahead of the kids and, being a larger than life Geordie, very few players would abuse their position. Those that did soon met the famous Roy look.

We were all devastated the day we heard they were told to vacate their room at the training ground. It was a cost cutting exercise, which I found difficult to comprehend, as they played a pivotal role in the development of players outside of football. Players over the years have commented on how Roy and Marie were like second parents and helped them through the emotional aspects of playing the game at such a young age. It's easy to forget that young players are under immense pressure to perform and to gain a professional contract. From a young age, normally 15 or 16, they have sacrificed their studies, friends and family to allow them the opportunity of becoming professional footballers. The rewards are such that I have personally seen young kids in tears when they have been refused a full time contract and told they are surplus to requirements. Such is the devastation it can take years to bring them back to the normality of life. For three years they are literally taken out of society in terms of cooking, working, paying the bills or even going out drinking every week. The pressure is constant, with regular fitness and development tests. An injury can finish your career before it has started. This is where Roy and Marie gave the kids the optimum chance of furthering their progress, be it at Coventry or another professional club. Their work was invaluable, yet the powers that be at Coventry could either not understand or were oblivious to their work and dedication.

At this point we were battling with the Council to move stadium. The situation was difficult as, years earlier, Bryan had sold Highfield Road to Wimpey's and they rented the stadium back to us for a fee. Crazily we probably ended up paying them more than they paid for the ground. We had no option but to move. I remember the fight going to the Council and the day of reckoning arrived. Mike, Graham and other members of staff went to the Council Chambers. A number of Councillors went through the motions. It was touch and go. The Labour leaders, some Lib Dems and the Socialist Party agreed to the move. Due to the overwhelming majority the club was granted a new stadium in Holbrooks. While I understood a move to a new state of the art stadium if we had full control of the revenue streams, I could not grasp moving where we were merely tenants. Senior colleagues of mine did bring this to the attention of the board on several occasions. Some were either reprimanded or in extreme cases fired. A new stadium, where we have no control of the naming rights, the stand sponsorships and catering, made no sense at all. The board were gambling the club's history, tradition and existence in a game of Russian roulette. I know of one particular Director who continuously challenged the board as he could see the new stadium did not make financial sense. He was eventually fired.

Rik leaving was a shock to us all, and at such a critical time. This was either a move to bring in an experienced Commercial Director to lead us to the new stadium or

Rik had upset the hierarchy. The one solace during these challenging times was when my second daughter Ria was born. Second time around I was ready and enjoyed the moment. When Simran was born I struggled with the prospect of becoming a father. It took me weeks before I came to terms with fatherhood. Of course I was full of joy, but not sure I was ready for parenthood so soon. The responsibility and the reality of life soon hits home when you become a parent. You become much more aware of your financial status and your career prospects. Kids are life changing and bring a new perspective on life. I can honestly say that the births of my kids changed me for the better. I had to grow up and quick. I was responsible for their welfare and had to start planning for the future.

After Rik's departure, a new Commercial Director was appointed – Mike McGinnity's friend, Alan Stevenson. He had extensive knowledge of the game as a former professional goalkeeper and Commercial Manager of WBA. Alan was brought in on the idea he would help generate additional revenue with ideas for when we left Highfield Road.

Alan was very commercially minded, which suited me, and he let me get on with new revenue ideas. He was also a close friend of Mike, which was a huge advantage when dealing with fellow colleagues and departments. Alan was old school in his way of thinking and working, but that suited me. If you worked hard you were rewarded and almost immediately Alan recognised the relationships I had built up with customers and let me continue with building the customer base. In some respects I was an excellent number two for Alan as I was for Rik. I ensured all the sponsorships and day to day running of the club was in order, and very rarely did we go without a sponsor or not have a full lounge for a match. The test was the less desirable matches on a Tuesday night. This allowed Rik and then Alan to focus on the bigger picture.

It appeared Alan was brought in to generate as much revenue as possible in the final season at Highfield Road, which he termed 'The end of an era'. It has to be one of the most enjoyable seasons I had experienced, with the buzz of a new stadium and being part of the management that said goodbye to our spiritual home. The desire to learn and take my world to new heights and continue to push the boundaries is the key to what motivates me. We all have ideas and aspirations; it's whether we are prepared to break the shackles and emancipate ourselves from the mental blocks we have embedded into us from a young age to reach the heights we are all capable of.

Since relegation there were many false dawns and excitement for the wrong reasons. One particular moment in September 2003 could have changed the landscape on the pitch. Gary McAllister, who was in charge at the time, was always looking to improve the team. Coventry had a good strong squad, though lacked a regular goalscorer. It's amazing how one poignant signing can change the dynamics of any team. We hear it all the time when managers say they are one signing away from creating a team capable of promotion. Well Coventry were minutes away from something special and a signing I genuinely believe would have had a positive impact on the team and the fans. I vividly remember Ravanelli in Bryan Richardson's office with Gary McAllister and agents galore representing Rava. I was with the press team waiting anxiously for the news we had signed Ravanelli. One minute it was a done deal, the next it was off. It was literally on and off for hours. Every so often Gary would walk into our office and you could tell by the look on his face how difficult and complicated the situation was. The Ravanelli signing should have been a formality; terms were allegedly agreed. The problem, as Gary kept highlighting, was Ravanelli's agents. He had to call several agents in various locations to approve the deal. It was not as straightforward as most transfers. Everybody wanted a piece of the cake. This was the first time I had heard of more than one party owning a player. The club had to seek approval from all the parties that owned a piece of Ravanelli, not to mention the split in agency fees. It was a no-win situation. You could see the frustration on the faces of Gary and Rava; he really wanted to play for Coventry. After hours of deliberation the deal fell through. We were so close yet so far from signing a marquee player who could have made a difference to our season.

There was so much anticipation on and off the pitch during the final season at Highfield Road. Naturally the outcome we all wanted was a team that could take us to the Premiership in time for the opening game at the Ricoh. This certainly would have made life off the pitch more interesting commercially. However, it's a well known fact that during the first season of a new stadium, clubs tend to find a significant increase in commercial revenues across the board. It's the feel good factor, expectation and wanting to be part of something historic. We are a nation of nostalgia. During pre-season at Highfield Road we found ourselves much busier than usual. Companies and individuals signed up to their respective lounges, boxes and other commercial deals earlier than normal. It was common practice for certain individuals and companies to agree the price and pay as late as possible. We knew them well and, to be fair, they always paid albeit last minute. They say life is a journey and during my time at Coventry I learnt so much about people and hope. Working at football clubs means you are dealing and negotiating with all types of companies and individuals, anything from your blue chip corporate to the one man bands. There were several decision makers I got to know that would always support me and my colleagues when in need of a sponsor for a particular match. Jimmy Spain from The Standard Triumph Club was a great example, and I have lost count of the number of times he would put his name to sponsoring matches. It was very simple with Jimmy. He would always turn up out of the blue to see me. There was no such thing as an appointment with Jimmy, and we didn't mind as he was such a decent person. After a while I would say to Jimmy we need a sponsor for a particular match. No problem, how much, Jimmy would ask in his broad Irish accent, couple of grand. Put me down that's fine. When's the game? Saturday, Jimmy. What day's it today, Thursday, Jimmy. Oh fuck, that's in two days, but I'll do it anyway. That was Jimmy Spain, god bless his soul, a kind, one-off gentleman.

Another great customer I eventually became close friends with was Kash from 21st Century Estate Agents. He was a straight-talking businessman who had a huge affinity with the club. He knew the challenges we were facing in the commercial department and how determined I was to ensure Coventry City Football Club was up there competing with the so-called bigger clubs. In football circles gaps commercially are quite embarrassing, especially when the opposite Chairman starts boasting about their finances and how great their commercial team is doing. Such exaggeration goes on all the time in boardrooms up and down the country. By the end of the match each Chairman has probably increased the commercial income tenfold. Each pre-season I would go and see Kash and offer him various sponsorships. His answer as always was yes, just invoice me. It got to the point at the end of each season I would have to explain what he had bought from me as he had no recollection. On numerous occasions Kash would just sign up for sponsorships and dinners without even checking his availability. This was a successful businessman, how could he not know? It transpired that as much as he wanted to help his beloved club, he also knew the pressure I was under to deliver. These are the moments and times you realise there is such a word as faith. There are some great people in this world who will go to any lengths to support others. Much of this was also borne out of the fact that, as a commercial team, we developed long term relationships with our customers. They felt part of the club.

The businesses and people of Coventry could not have done any more for us. I know of Company Directors who over-budgeted just to help the club. People who come to mind who always supported us in any way they could included David Shortland, Geoff Harris from Coventry Heating & Plumbing Supplies, Kash from 21st Century Estate Agents, Tony McGurk, Tony Banger Walsh, Eamonn & Ian from Hose and Engineering, Rob Ally from XL Motors and Moe Kandola from the Bedford Street Bar (Leamington), just too many to name. Since working at clubs up and down the UK I have realised every club and every city will have such individuals in their midst. All they asked for was to be treated with respect. One particular person I have always remained in touch with is Randi Weaver. While at Coventry we used to receive a call each season to sponsor one of the local players in the match day programme. The problem was nobody knew who this person was. If we ever needed support with sponsorship we would call Randi and 99% of the time she would help the club. This went on for several seasons and yet nobody had ever met Randi. In some ways she wanted to remain anonymous and not be made a fuss of. I was curious as to who this person really was. A few years later I had the pleasure to meet Randi and it transpired she was a senior executive of a big American finance company. Having met Randi you would never know how successful she is. She was so humble and down to earth. Randi and Noel Hand are some of the first people I speak to when I look for advice. No matter what support I ask of Randi she never says no.

The point here, as in other sections of this book, is that we do have successful people who are prepared to help. If we can replicate their good work and do the same for others, imagine the positive vibe we could all create. It probably sounds like a religious sermon, but if we can face our own fears we may just find a lifetime of happiness. I have tried at all the clubs I have been lucky to represent to adopt my unique methods of giving something back to individuals and businesses. When you are giving you are at your best.

Randi Weaver and Noel Hand, who I have mentioned earlier, and several others have been instrumental in my career. They would offer me advice and share their thoughts on how to win and keep business. Their methods were simple yet effective. Noel was costing companies thousands of pounds to coach sales techniques, yet here he was, constantly advising and supporting me to improve me as a person. He also realised I wanted to learn. I always strived to better myself, and what better opportunity than to learn from those who are successful and prepared to help? The advice he and many other Coventry companies and individuals have given me has been invaluable.

It was during this particular period that I began to understand human behaviour and how people react to given stimuli. I have always wanted to learn and continue to improve myself as a person and professional. For the first time the emphasis shifted from selling the football to presenting opportunities to businesses without actually discussing the football.

From early 2000s the emphasis once again moved to global partnerships. Very few of the top clubs adopted this new revenue stream at the time and have to be congratulated for having such foresight. At Coventry we were discussing such opportunities during the late 90s, though this fizzled out as we could not attract support from the top and several of the Directors at the time felt we should focus on the local and regional areas. We already had a team working with local companies – what we needed was to reach out to global organisations that wanted to break into English football. Exciting times at Coventry for me were during the mid nineties to around 2005. The club still had a family feel and many of the staff had been at Coventry for a number of years. It was very rare to see anyone leave unless they had an offer they could not refuse. Football clubs behind the scenes epitomised my experiences at Coventry. They really were family affairs. Nepotism is taking it a little too far, but if an administration position was available it was usually filled by someone we knew.

The final year at Highfield Road had all the attributes you expect moving from a ground graced by some of the best footballers for over 100 years. While the 2004/05 season was once again a typical Sky Blues year of hope, anticipation and back to the drawing board, there was an amazing finale for the history books. The last ever game at Highfield Road was against Derby County and how poignant that one of our heroes, Mo Konjic, was on the opposition side, though at times during the game you sensed he forgot which side he was playing for. The build up had been intense for weeks. The place was totally sold out for the game. With many of the Sky Blue heroes returning for the match, this was going to be one hell of an emotional rollercoaster. The team just had to perform on the pitch and the pressure was on to leave Highfield Road with a bang. This was history in the making and to be fair the team did the club and city proud on the day. Due to all the seats being sold out, me and the rest of the commercial team took our place on the roof of the PA room, which was situated in the middle of the dug outs.

This was the only place we could watch the game and probably had the best view. No one appeared to care, even though we broke all the health and safety rules. There was absolutely no way I was missing this game for anyone. I remember the sun shining and thinking this is going to be our day. Our day it certainly was, as we hammered the Rams 6-2. Coventry kid Gary McSheffrey started the rout with two goals in succession and by half-time we were leading 4-0. The second half was just as exciting and even though Derby pulled a couple of goals back, Coventry went on to score two more with Andy Whing scoring the last ever goal at Highfield Road. At the final whistle Sky Blue fans invaded the pitch and what I remember is Jimmy Hill taking to the microphone to sing the famous Sky Blue song with over 20,000 joining in. The emotions were high, with Bobby Gould and many other former greats in tears. That evening I joined John Sillett and many other Sky Blues legends for drinks in the Vice Presidents Club. Not sure who was paying but the drinks were free flowing. This was a magic moment and as a Coventry City fan I looked forward to the future. The end was here, as we were about to embark on a new chapter in a new stadium purposely built for Coventry City Football Club!

Many of the staff moving to the new stadium were full of anticipation, excitement, doubt, fear; it all existed. Rather than look back, moving to the new stadium was going to be a new journey in my career.

Once the new stadium was complete and the honeymoon period was over there was a task of now fulfilling the business obligations of the club. We had almost 3-4 times more space to fill with clients and as many advertising opportunities. Naturally the final season at Highfield Road was used to sell the dream to clients and, with the experience of Alan, was completed very well. Businesses that I never even knew existed came out of the woodwork and became members without any persuasion. Admittedly we did have a handicap with the all new Premier Club, a concept brought to this country from Australia and implemented with precision by Ken Sharp, who is a theoretical genius.

The deal struck by the management at Coventry City was that we could not sell any of our suites or Executive boxes to new clients. We could not even approach new clients until a month before the opening of the new stadium. Imagine having 3-4 times as much to sell and being restricted to sell any inventory until a month before the official opening. This was a mammoth task, almost impossible. Well, we made the impossible possible by developing new avenues of generating leads which did not contravene the contract set by the Premier Club and the club. Rather than make excuses, we found a loophole and made the best of it. I fully understood the agreement in place for the Premier Club was to encourage businesses to purchase five-year debenture seats as opposed to one year deals we were offering. It made business sense. What did not make sense were the senior board members expecting us to sell our commercial areas within a month. This was totally unreasonable. Once again the commercial team were persistent, had belief and had the courage to make it happen. Make it happen we did; all executive boxes sold out and 2 of the 3 lounges were at the capacity and remained as such until I departed for Watford Football Club two years later. The 2005/06 season started with several away games, as the Ricoh was not ready. The first home game was against QPR with a limited capacity of 23,000 which sold out. It was touch and go whether the game would go ahead. We were told to just continue as normal. Two thousand corporate customers were descending upon the Ricoh and we were not even granted a safety licence. Fortunately, at the last minute, we were given the green light. Lady luck was on our side as we were clearly not ready and there was much work still to complete. The game itself was a spectacle as we beat QPR 3-0.

It was apparent that there were major financial issues at the club, with many of the senior management now leaving their posts by way of redundancy and compromise agreements. This all seemed too ominous. The problem with football clubs is too often senior personnel are employed with an excellent knowledge of their own business and yet very little specialist knowledge of the football industry. With little or no football specific knowledge, more often than not they make the same mistakes as their predecessors and the club very quickly becomes embroiled in debt or worse still mismanagement. What they need are senior mentors from their club or the football industry to guide them.

This was certainly the case at Coventry, with particular people being employed due to their association with Bryan Richardson. They were probably very successful in their respective areas of expertise. As they found out soon, the business of football was unique and needed a different type of mindset to a normal business practice. It was during the first season at the Ricoh that we encountered problems internally and externally. We officially moved to the new stadium from Highfield Road in September and had the offices directly opposite the dual carriageway. The offices were pertinent to our requirements. However, by October there were changes again, with many of the senior team now removed and the introduction of the new management team consisting of Geoffrey Robinson, Paul Fletcher as CEO, Ken Sharp as Commercial Director and Mal Brannigan as Financial Director.

Admittedly I was fearful for my own position, as I heard Ken was appointing his own Sales Manager. The club did not require a Sales and Commercial Manager as the roles overlapped. Once again for some reason I was optimistic after all the doubts and fears. I had this intuition that I would be fine. Be it education, work or other areas of my life, I have always encountered doubt, fear and indecision eventually followed by an overwhelming sense of optimism. One of the many lessons I learned was to plan your own destiny and fate. Luck does not exist – it's how proactive and determined you are that dictates your life. The age old phrase of you are what you think about all day is so true.

NEW OWNERS, NEW ERA

The first season under the stewardship of Paul Fletcher was interesting. He was talking about the football club achieving Premiership status within 3 years or he would resign. This was an incredible statement – was he serious or was it a circus coming to town? Admittedly, the first few months were difficult for me with a Sales Manager in place and me feeling a sense of isolation. Ken had many projects on the go which, if successful, would benefit the club enormously. At this stage I was unsure of the whole project. This had more to do with the fact that I was out of my comfort zone. It was only after Paul and Ken left for pastures new that I realised we had some of the most visionary guys at our club. I also had an excellent rapport with Mal, Ken and Paul, who are some of the most honest and credible guys to work with in football. We are good friends – positive people will always remain and stick together. After all these years, I still call Ken and Paul for any advice. That is how high I rate these guys.

What was achieved under Paul was incredible and was one of the most enjoyable times of my career, without even knowing it at the time. Paul would constantly tell us all we can do what we want. One of the first things he did when he arrived was to provide all the staff with a desk sign stating 'if what I am doing is not productive for the club why am I doing it?' Admittedly, we all found this strange and criticised Paul. What was beyond us was how powerful the message was. Every member of staff had a meeting with Paul discussing any concerns at the club and how they could be improved personally and professionally. These were good times and we didn't even realise it.

During the first 12 months we were launching a series of initiatives. All were relatively successful. It was only years later when I was having a drink one day with Paul that he admitted I was meant to be fired when the new Sales Manager arrived. However Paul refused to do so and, in time, he understood my worth to the club with the amount of revenue I was generating into the club. This is a true mark of a manager.

Paul was also instrumental in me moving to Watford. Deciding to move was a huge decision for me. For two to three years earlier I was constantly thinking about whether I could achieve the same success at another club. This always played on my mind. Did I really have what it takes? After only two months of the new owners, Sisu, taking over at Coventry, I made the important decision of moving on. I vividly remember Joe Elliott walking in to the offices and declaring he had finally signed a deal to save the club from administration. We were on the brink and at the time this was a relief to us all. When I started to look into the new ownership I realised they were a hedge fund group with Ray Ranson fronting the consortium. Ray was a football man, so surely this would be to our advantage. The early days were a nervous time for us all with so many people representing the new owners coming and going from the offices. Unlike when Paul, Mal and Ken joined, I was unsure of the future this time around. The Coventry Telegraph was called to take a staff photograph celebrating the news of a takeover. Outside the offices all the staff were asked to jump in the air to show how appreciative we were. I was the only one not to jump; firstly it would make me look like a dick and, secondly, my intuition was making me uncomfortable about the new ownership.

I was feeling vulnerable. I remember speaking to my brother Sonny later that day and saying this deal is not all that it seems. I had no proof or any dealings with the new owners. For some reason I just did not feel comfortable. Mal, who continued as a Financial Director, assured me this could be great for the city. He was right to a point, as we had avoided administration. What occurred over the next few weeks and months convinced me it was time to leave. I saw Mal as a friend of mine who played a huge part in getting the deal over the line and was suddenly released. I just remember him coming over to see me and this person is a man's man, but he had tears in his eyes. He had been deceived by a certain person at the club. When all the information had been extracted from him he was gone. That's life to some people, but to me it's wrong. Let people leave with respect and dignity.

The new owners wanted full control and to do so needed to acquire a certain percentage of shares to become a private entity. There are arguments for and against, though at that time they had big plans and wanted to take Coventry back to the Premiership. This is all I was hearing from Ray and I believed him. With investment and a successful team on the pitch the revenue would certainly flow into the coffers. Firstly there was to be an overhaul of the club on and off the pitch. In the first few weeks the new management went about collecting shares. I had some shares that a customer had given me. The shares simply gave me a piece of the club and that's all they were for me. As the shares started rolling in a colleague who worked in the finance department mentioned it would be a good idea for me to personally hand my few shares in. Reluctantly I did and thought I was playing my part in Coventry City's new future. I handed my shares to an appointed accountant on behalf of the new owners. Not even a thank you. In fact she did not even acknowledge me. That moment I made my mind up of what we were dealing with and it wasn't going to be pleasant. Still knowing this, I refused to deal with my career aspirations. Now was the time to move on and challenge myself at another club. I just could not do it and kept looking for excuses. I was scared of leaving Coventry City Football Club; this is all I knew.

Fear, doubt, indecision dominated my thoughts. These powerful negative thoughts were controlling my life and I was allowing it to happen. To make matters worse, not everyone had caved in and handed their shares in. The club needed a big name to get the momentum going. I was very good friends with Jimmy and Bryony Hill and many at the club knew this. I had no agenda and whenever I called Jimmy it was to support my projects at Coventry City and not for personal gain. If the club could persuade Jimmy to hand over his shares they would have a coup. I was asked by a certain Director to help. I called Jimmy and Bryony and explained the situation. Jimmy was happy to do so in the knowledge it was for the good of Coventry City Football Club.

On New Year's Eve Joe Elliott and I made our way to Hurstpierpoint, near Brighton, to see Jimmy Hill and collect his shares. I had been to Jimmy's home before and so knew the way but this was New Year's Eve and the club were determined to collect the shares as soon as possible. It was also a three hour journey. We didn't stay long and after lunch made our way back. On our return we headed straight to the Coventry Telegraph offices, where Andy Turner was waiting to write the story. Hindsight is a wonderful thought and if I knew then what I know now I would never have gone, irrespective of the situation. I am not saying for one moment Jimmy Hill handed his shares over because of me, but he loves the club like us all and wanted to play his part in its future. He had several conversations with Directors and had made his mind up during those calls. New Year's Eve was a formality.

The last time I visited Jimmy was for a club promotion regarding Operation Premiership. Paul Fletcher knew about my friendship with Jimmy and so asked me to accompany the press team. It was during this visit that Jimmy Hill opened up about his time at Coventry.

While Dan from the media team was still having lunch, Jimmy and I sat in his lounge which had a huge log fire burning away. Intrigued about the Sky Blue Revolution during his time there I asked him several questions relating to him leaving when he did and what he could have achieved if he had remained at Coventry. At first he was coy but then he just opened up. Jimmy clearly stated that if he had his time again he would have remained with Coventry for a couple more seasons to see how far he could have taken them in Division 1. He genuinely believed the team he left was good enough to compete for Europe for several years. He had created a club that had a conveyor belt of young talented players emerging each season. When pushed, he felt he would have produced a team good enough to challenge for Division 1. At that stage I nearly fell off my chair. Coventry City to challenge for the top league! Jimmy was confident Coventry City would have been a top six club competing for honours on a regular basis.

Jimmy showed me pictures of him photographed with famous celebrities and models from across the world. He had the charm and charisma and was a celebrity in his own right. Unfortunately for Coventry City he made a decision which was great for Jimmy but leaves several question marks for the club and what he could have achieved if he had stayed and turned down ITV.

Jimmy was in full flow about his time at Coventry and how he would release players when many felt they were at their peak. He explained his philosophy that he would sell a player when he felt they had reached a particular tipping point. He just knew when a player was at his peak for the club and could do no more. He was quite detailed about his theory, though I didn't quite understand the concept, though agreed nevertheless. After a while Jimmy just went quiet and stared into space – he was in deep profound thought. He changed the topic and we spoke about other things; he never returned to the subject of Coventry City again. As a Coventry supporter I left his house thinking what if?

Back to reality and at this stage it must be stated that, while I had my reservations, the new owners had saved the club from administration. We needed to work with them. From a personal point of view I needed to know whether my position would be affected. It's human nature to look after the wellbeing of your family. Weeks after Sisu had acquired the set number of shares we were all called to a meeting. Ray addressed all the staff to explain there was a need for a reorganisation and redundancies would be inevitable. On one hand we have been saved and on the other we are about to lose good, loyal employees. That's the harsh reality of life, I thought. In the coming weeks we all received letters explaining the restructure and how it would affect our own positions. It's never a great position to be in, though at the time I believed these great business brains to have a master plan. Surely they know what they are doing. After all, they were successful people in their own right. What football has taught me is that in this industry you are dealing with an animal that you cannot control and dictate to. You need experienced knowledgeable people to tame the animal, but you can never control it. One by one, experienced staff were made redundant or either decided to take voluntary redundancy or leave for new positions at other clubs. This is the moment, in my opinion, the fabric of the club was destroyed. The heart of the club was ripped out and would resonate in years to come. Employees with years of experience, knowledge and Coventry in their hearts and minds were being thrown onto the scrapheap. They were not just friends – we were like a family. Many of the older employees, who only knew Coventry City, were distraught – this was their life and they had given everything to the cause. In a matter of months the heartbeat of Coventry City Football Club was destroyed. It was only a matter of time before the club was brought to its knees by a ruthless regime oblivious to the football industry and a city that looks after its own.

I have heard the phrase dead wood so often during my time in football. What exactly is dead wood, I would consistently ask the HR consultant at Coventry? For me it's an excuse to remove people who do not fit into an organisation's plans. As harsh as it may seem, I can understand moving employees on if they do not accept change or agree with the strategy of an organisation moving forward. This can only end up being harmful to both the organisation and the employees in question. However, to remove employees with no appropriate reason other than the fact they have been loyal for so many years is a futile excuse. Knowledge and experience is invaluable, and so often I have seen organisations make the same mistake and then find themselves in the wilderness wondering what went wrong. You let your assets go, that's what went wrong. The wind of change was blowing and I didn't like the direction it was heading. I was undecided and thought of fighting for my role rather than leave. Remember I was in my comfort zone and did not have the confidence or temerity to leave, which is the real reason I stayed.

From March onwards all employees were in a state of uncertainty. This was a period of major restructuring for the club. We had received new job roles with several positions downgraded. Naturally this meant a restructure of the actual job description and the remuneration package. All the positions being restructured could be applied for by anyone in the club. In reality the person who was actually performing the role would be offered the position, this was just a tick in the HR box in my opinion.

My interview was comical. Walking into the meeting room I was greeted by the Head of HR and the new Finance Director for Coventry City FC. The interview was a formality, as they both had no idea of what my position entailed. There was a series of general questions which I answered and the interview was over after twenty minutes or so. In my opinion the club knew exactly who was staying and going before the interviews were held. During a home fixture I was tipped off by a Club Director that my position was safe. What he failed to tell me was that they were reducing my overall package, which was not in line with similar positions to begin with. I knew deep down that my time at Coventry was coming to an end. In my capacity to bring new customers and revenue to the club I previously had use of a company car. A decision was made soon after to replace company cars with lease cars. This was normal practice at many organisations and was beneficial for tax purposes. Unfortunately the Head of PR and I were told we had to fund our own transport. We both found this incredulous, as they were taking away the tools pertinent to doing our jobs efficiently. To add insult to injury we later discovered certain members of staff were offered contracts which included funds to lease a car. They were on a similar scale to us, had no interaction with customers and never needed to leave the office.

The writing was clearly on the wall of who was required and who was not. The only issue was the current incumbents had never managed a club and were working to a philosophy I believe could only fail. On match-days everything worked like clockwork. Customers were greeted at the entrance and I ensured I met as many customers as possible. We had volunteers, such as Dave Cleobury, who would literally help wherever we needed him. People like him and many others contributed to the success of match days, though this was never really appreciated by the new management. The volunteers were Coventry through and through. Times were changing and I could visualise the impact on my career if I remained. After careful consideration, I decided to move on. This was the only way to get out of the rut that I was stuck in. I was not enjoying my time at the club. Coventry City Football Club was unrecognisable. The truth was that Coventry City was going through a transitional period prior to Sisu joining. Change was inevitable and it was time for me to get out of my comfort zone and find new employment.

My mind was truly made up; I was leaving after almost fourteen years. Once again I planned my move by deciding which clubs I would like to work with and then contacting the owners directly. This had worked before, it would work again. During my time in sales I realised most, if not all, people fail to contact the decision maker. Most of the time they approach HR, who in most cases tend to react to the requirements of the club.

I remember contacting and speaking to Amit Bhatia directly. He was one of the owners of Queens Park Rangers and the son-in-law of the billionaire steel tycoon Lakshmi Mittal. He was only human after all; it's just that we tend to put people of a certain disposition on a pedestal and treat them as such. Like Gordon Strachan once said to me we are all equal, as we all crap down the same pan.

I actually got quite far down the line at QPR, as Amit asked me to contact the new Commercial Director at QPR. Unfortunately, and for whatever reason, the Commercial Director refused to take our conversations any further. I then contacted the Sales and Marketing Director at Wolverhampton Wanderers, who told me he was in the process of leaving and could I forward my CV on to him. Forty minutes later I was outside his office to personally deliver my CV. Impressed, he interviewed me there and then. He later put me forward to the final interview with the CEO. At this time I also received a call from Julian Winter, the Deputy CEO at Watford and from the CEO at MK Dons.

MK Dons was in fact a disaster, as the new CEO had absolutely no clue about the commercial world of football. He had no idea or understanding of my presentation and I actually could sense he felt threatened. I just knew this had gone wrong. Needless to say he did not proceed with inviting me back for a second interview but had the cheek to ask for my presentation. My interview with the Wolverhampton CEO arrived and for some unknown reason a sense of fear overcame me. Meeting Jez Moxey for the first time was quite daunting as he has a fantastic and equally fearsome reputation in the football industry. For some reason I did not perform, even though I knew the job could be mine if I really wanted it. Jez kept asking me to tell him why I wanted the job. However my heart was telling me this was not for me. I not only bottled it, I gave a sterling performance in how not to get hired.

I knew I had Watford to potentially fall back on. When I met Julian I have to say I knew this was the club for me. He has to be one of the most honest and credible Senior Managers I have ever had the pleasure to work with. He trusts you to get on with your job and, like Paul Fletcher, lets you manage.

Fortunately, Julian and I really got on and I made it to the next stage of interviews. The second interview was to meet Mark Ashton, CEO of Watford. I remember meeting Mark, who was full of enthusiasm of what he had achieved at Watford in a short space of time. Everything was positive. I left the interview full of expectation that this really was the club for me. Much further than Wolves but the club for me; I just had this feeling Watford was the right club.

After a brief hiatus Julian contacted me to meet him along with Mark and the Chairman. At this stage I really wanted out of Coventry.

I remember travelling to Watford with Sharon driving as I had no transport. Once there we were both asked to meet the senior management team. This was the club for me and I really wanted the position. We met in the Chairman's office; I felt proud and valued. Had my time come?

Mark offered me the role but I said I needed time think about it – think about it! This was my chance. For some reason I had this overwhelming urge to have the weekend to make a decision. I already knew I wanted the position, what was to think about? I genuinely believe Mark thought I was negotiating and said we will pay you whatever you want if you take the role today. Before I could even blink my wife was already shaking hands with the Chairman saying I would take the position! The next stage was for me to state what I wanted. I had a figure in my head and told Julian what I wanted. Incredibly he had the same figure written down; talk about creating my fate. The deal was done – I was now officially moving to Watford Football Club. Yet you would never have guessed it. Driving back to Coventry both Sharon and I were quiet, perhaps in disbelief that I had been offered a life-changing opportunity. I had also spent almost fourteen years at Coventry and knew no other employer. I had been in my comfort zone far too long. It was so surreal that we ended up at Shimla Spice, a curry house near Coventry Railway Station, discussing whether I had made the right decision or not. These were natural human fears of what if? By the Monday the what if's had disappeared. My best friend and close companion in life called belief had returned. A new chapter and journey was about to begin.

M1 TO WATFORD

I finished work at Coventry City on Tuesday and had arranged a small get together that evening with colleagues and friends. I am not ashamed to admit I cried my eyes out when I finally walked away, as the club had played a huge part in my life. No respite and no time to think about my new position. I began my new role at Watford on the Wednesday. The drive to and from Watford was to become my life for the next four years. The M1 almost felt like a personal friend. I spent more time on the M1 than in my own home!

On my first day at Watford FC I noticed how plush the offices were. What immediately struck me was the community department positioned right in the middle of the offices. They were central and at the heart of everything Watford stood for which is testament to what Graham Taylor had created several years earlier. Staff had been relocated the previous season due to major building work at Vicarage Road. In essence I had moved to a smaller club than Coventry and to an old ground in need of improvement. My first day entailed a visit to Vicarage Road and I must admit it felt strange working for a club that had a three-sided ground. I guess moving from the Ricoh was always going to have an impact. However, I could move away from the reality of Vicarage Road as I was situated in the luxury offices only two miles away in Rickmansworth. The facilities at Vicarage Road were smaller in comparison to Highfield Road and parts of the ground in need of major renovation. The dressing rooms were almost untouched from Graham Taylor's first stint at the club. The home and away dressing rooms were a typical throwback to the 70s and 80s with a few mod cons thrown in to make it feel slightly contemporary, but in reality nothing could improve the dressing rooms unless they were totally refurbished. Like most professional clubs you could feel the history and tradition when standing in the home dressing room. It had a presence. The old gym behind the physio's room still had some of the old furniture and to think this is where players of the calibre of John Barnes, Luther Blissett and many of the well-known Watford teams were based makes you realise how much the game has moved on. The gym was clearly out of use, as the club had a state of the art training ground at Colney directly next door to where Arsenal trained. Adjacent to the dressing room area were several rooms that once occupied the Directors and their guests. This was now completely closed due to health and safety reasons, though the original fixtures and fittings were still intact. This was history that had become lost. Several years later Neil Price, a former player, and I discovered a room full of old pictures and trophies. Some of the pictures were from the 1900s and yet here they were gathering dust. We did bring this to the attention of the board and requested a room or a convenient safe place where such items could be on show for all supporters to see. I just hope the club have found a place to exhibit such history for supporters and those interested in the club.

The first three days were a learning curve. I had no experience of moving to another club and quite frankly I was nervous. While I was expected to make steady progress I put added pressure on myself by deciding I had to make an immediate impact. My attitude was ridiculous, as it can take weeks if not months to implement plans and strategies. I decided to firstly observe the culture of the club and make a mental note of the politically important people. There are normally a select group of people in any organisation who can be quite influential in decision making. It's about understanding the dynamics of any organisation if you are to progress and have a productive time at work.

Meeting your team and all the staff can take several days. Then there's a small issue of remembering the names of everyone you have met. The weekend could not arrive quickly enough though. This gave me the time to reflect on what I needed to do. I wrote down all the basic principles of what we developed at Coventry and merely replicated the template. For the first time I was the one making decisions for the commercial department; the responsibility all laid with me. This thought alone drove me on, as I genuinely wanted to make a go of it for the club and for personal reasons. Watford was a family club and I felt this from the day I started. The people here cared for their club and that really impressed me.

I remember meeting my sales staff for the first time and it struck me how low on confidence they were. In essence they lacked motivation. Over the next few weeks I had one to one meetings and worked closely with them. I noticed a remarkable difference in their appearance and attitude. The results also improved. Rather than be critical, I led a positive approach and made them feel valued. As humans we all react to positive feedback, which results in productive people. Those who make a decision not to co-operate tend to eventually move on.

I was full of enthusiasm as I drove to Watford on the Monday morning, three days after joining. The town could not come fast enough; my head was full of ideas. I was buzzing with positivity. Several of my most creative ideas were born during my long trips to and from Watford. On my arrival that Monday morning I wrote out our targets; this was our team and we were going to do the best we could while enjoying the journey. Time would tell how we fared.

One of the challenges at Watford was to attract new investment and engage with local organisations. Being so close to London posed its own problems, as it was just as easy to support some of the established Premiership clubs such as Chelsea, Arsenal and Spurs. This was also Watford's second season in the Championship after losing in the first round of the play-off. I knew my experience and the business template we employed at Coventry would eventually come good. In the meantime I was tasked with a major situation in only my first couple of weeks. As with all football clubs, one of the major income streams is the front of shirt sponsorship. For clubs outside of the Premiership sourcing a new shirt sponsorship can be a difficult and arduous process as you are dealing with the reality of what someone is prepared to pay compared to the Chairman's figure, which most of the time can be worlds apart. As my luck would have it Watford were in the final year of their deal with Beko. I still remember the moment I was told that left me thinking shit, here we go again. The truth of the matter is there is not a long list of companies waiting to sponsor your club shirt outside of the Premiership, and the disparity between the price of the Premiership and Championship is monumental. Whereas clubs in the Premiership can command millions of pounds per season, in the Championship anything over £200k is considered a good deal.

Those who work in the football industry will understand the need to secure a shirt sponsor before Christmas so you can launch the shirts during the close season, capitalising on kids' holidays. When clubs launch their shirts late this is not due to a lack of foresight of the Retail Manager. Normally this is due to the lateness of securing a shirt sponsor, which in turn means the club in question has to wait months for the shirts to be manufactured. Due to the high costs of manufacturing in the UK most of the big brands operate in China. As with most goods from that part of the continent, shipping has to be booked several months in advance. This can be a major process and not as easy as manufacturing shirts one week and having them delivered the next. In reality a shirt should be signed off by the end of October. Only then are you guaranteed to receive your shirts the following May. The critical period is based on 6/7 months.

The months from July to December were turbulent off the pitch. You could feel the uncertainty amongst the Chairman and CEO. This naturally filters down to the senior management and staff. I sensed there was a problem, though never really asked any questions as I was just trying to focus on my own role. The team were struggling on the pitch and the team manager Aidy Boothroyd's visits to the office became less frequent. It doesn't take a genius to work out there were issues brewing off the pitch. Due to a poor start to the season and with the supporters openly venting their fury Aidy was finally dismissed. There were rumours, as expected, of who was going to take over. When the announcement was eventually made most of the staff including me had never heard of the new manager. Over the next few months we were all raving about our new signing.

The club had signed a little-known manager by the name of Brendan Rodgers. The first time I met Brendan I found him to be an affable guy and had this presence about him. What also struck me was his ability to make people feel at ease. This was after all a manager who had spent quality time with Jose Mourinho. During his brief tenure Brendan had his team playing some of the most attractive football we had seen at Vicarage Road for some years. It was only a matter of time before clubs with a bigger playing budget came knocking and come knocking they did, as Brendan moved on to Reading, Swansea and then Liverpool where he almost won the Premiership title.

As mentioned earlier you could sense all was not right off the pitch and all this came to a head immediately after Christmas at the annual AGM. The Watford Chairman Graham Simpson resigned. The resignation of the Chairman was a surprise, as he was defiant before the AGM he would continue. However, at the AGM there was a brief discussion between him and shareholders Jimmy and Vince Russo. I'm not sure what was said to this day, he simply resigned that evening. I never heard from him again.

Over the next few days it was announced Jimmy Russo would be installed as Chairman along with his brother Vince Russo in an advisory capacity. There were many Watford employees who welcomed the new custodians, though there were also a minority who were suspicious and had a loyalty to the previous Chairman. I was still fairly new to the club and had no real allegiances either way. I was here to perform a role and would do so under any stewardship.

Under the leadership of Jimmy and Vince I actually had one of the most enjoyable times of my career. They were both down to earth people, unpretentious and we hit it off immediately. The first time Jimmy visited the club he spoke to all the staff and introduced himself to those who were new to the club. He had a huge personality and could win anyone over with his enthusiasm and passion for the game. You felt at ease with Jimmy and he gave you the confidence to share your thoughts irrespective of whether he agreed with you or not, though the way the previous Chairman disappeared I made sure I agreed with him. Vince was the quieter of the two – almost a good cop bad cop scenario. I didn't care which role the brothers were playing – I certainly wasn't getting on the wrong side of these guys.

In all my time in football Jimmy and Vince for me were the dream owners and employers where you had the freedom and confidence to push the boundaries. But you made sure they agreed to the boundaries first!

I understood their psyche. Sons of working class Italian immigrants, they had to start from the bottom and work their way to the top and so knew the value of a pound. To achieve at the highest level you have to take risks and fear what you may not achieve as opposed to fearing to try. They had built up a multi-million pound fruit and vegetable business in Essex, supplying to all the major brands in the UK and abroad. In many ways I resonated with Jimmy and Vince knowing the difficulties my parents had when they first arrived in the UK. This is why many second and third generation kids' of immigrant families generally do well as they are continuously pushed 24/7 to achieve an education to improve their opportunities in life. Put me in a business situation and I will make money all day long. We all have our niche in life. From day one, whenever Jimmy or Vince would arrive at the Watford offices they would make a point of greeting all the employees. There were no airs and graces with the brothers.

In my experience most of the Chairmen I have worked with will not have the same employee/Chairman relationship. For some reason certain people at the very top create a situation of us and them. Perhaps it has something to do with gaining respect or an ego boost. What they fail to realise is that an engaged workforce is much more productive and creates a happier atmosphere. I am not aware of a single business manual that encourages Senior Managers or leaders to keep a distance from their staff. You can be professional and develop a fantastic rapport with your employees, who are there to serve you and your organisation. Employees can see right through Senior Managers when times are bad, hence the need for a hands on leader at the top. Even though Jimmy and Vince had their doubters at the club due to previous experiences, I could see the benefit they would bring to the club.

Jimmy in particular had a presence about him and his dress sense was impeccable. How people dressed was important to Jimmy and he made several positive comments on my dress sense as I invested in several suits to look sharp. Unfortunately some of the suits I had purchased were clearly impulse buys as at times it appeared I had worn them for a bet! I have always tried to look pristine and make an effort, as I have been drilled by my father about how one should look at all times. One time I remember Jimmy and I having a conversation about how a person should look and dress. He explained a man should have three quality items, a suit, shoes and a watch. He reminded me of exactly what my father told me some years earlier.

Such were Jimmy and Vince's reputations some of the staff believed they had connections with the mafia, which was total nonsense. I am sure many of the board nervously disagreed with them on certain club issues not knowing whether they would find a horse's head in their bed the next day! I almost believed the hype one day when Vince asked me to meet him in the staff car park along with my car keys. He wanted to discreetly put something in my boot. My mind was racing as to what he wanted to put in my car boot. What if it was illegal goods? I began thinking of excuses and at one point must have said it's against my religion to accept gifts on a Friday. He did stare at me for a few seconds then carried on as if he misheard me. He asked me to remain quiet and not tell anyone what he was about to give me. I was really shitting it at this stage. Then he slowly opened his boot and to my relief there in front of me were bottles of legitimate Italian wine. I gave out a huge sigh while hugging Vince at the same time, which put him out of his comfort zone and not sure he's ever been right since. After that escapade he never offered me any Italian wines again. In fact he never spoke to me again and only nodded whenever our paths crossed.

On the pitch the team performed well under the stewardship of new manager Brendan Rodgers. Even then you could tell he was a great man manger and always made time for all the staff and not just the players. A great psychologist, he brought the best out of the players. To think at the time his backroom staff consisted of Malky McKay and Sean Dyche. All from the same school of thought, I for one am not surprised at the success they have brought to their respective clubs. Malky McKay, who was Brendan's assistant and second in command, was offered the manager's position when Brendan moved on and interestingly Sean Dyche moved up as Malky's assistant. These two were superb football coaches and people. I got on very well with Malky and Sean and stay in touch with them to this day. Watford, as expected, received several quality CVs though the board felt Malky deserved his opportunity and rightly so. There was always going to be a cynicism with Malky being offered the job and cries of a cheap option were always touted about. The truth is Malky was the best man for the job and proved himself during the interview process. Let's not forget the great Graham Taylor was on the interviewing panel.

I had a great relationship with Malky, who was always positive. I remember one particular afternoon where we sat for hours in his office discussing the subject of psychology and the impact it can have on your lives. We could have been in some lecture at University such was the profoundness of our conversation. Malky was an extremely clever person. We were so engrossed in our conversation Malky forgot he had arranged a meeting with Danny Graham, one of the players. Danny popped his head around and mentioned he was waiting outside. To my surprise Malky just cancelled the meeting with Danny and we kept on talking about life in general. I must have made a small impression. Due to being a late starter in football he appreciated his opportunity. He also wrote his goals and objectives down and aspired to achieve them. I found this fascinating as that is exactly what I had been doing for several years. During the conversation I mentioned to Malky that, being ambitious himself, surely he would harbour aspirations to move on to a potentially bigger project than Watford. He smiled though revealed nothing. Suffice to say Malky was unveiled as the Cardiff City manager months later. We have remained good friends and Malky was also instrumental in me joining Glasgow Rangers. I called him before my interview and he just sold the club and city to me and explained that opportunities to work for clubs such as Rangers are rare and when offered the chance to take it.

Talking about pressure off the pitch, we were into February without a front of shirt sponsor. The Board of Directors tried to provide support by contacting decision makers they personally knew but to no avail. We were now at panic stations. It became so bad we were literally complaining about the shirt designs with the manufacturer to stall them for as long as possible. In the meantime I remember driving up and down the motorway determined to find a suitable sponsor. We did receive two offers; however they were rejected. One of the offers came when I contacted a local logistics company. They offered a six figure sum on a three year deal. The caveat to the deal was the owner wanted two places in the boardroom for all home matches for the duration of the contract. Jimmy & Vince refused the deal as they felt the offer did not warrant boardroom places. I believe there was more to this, as Jimmy appeared to know the people in question, but never revealed anything to me. As desperate as I was to source a sponsor on this occasion even I decided it was best not to ask any questions!

With time literally running out we eventually found a shirt sponsor in Evolution, a company I was introduced to by a friend and ex-professional footballer Kirk Stephens. A decision had to be made immediately and with no other offer on the table and after rejecting a good proposal we took the risk. The owner as it soon transpired was nothing more than a real life Walter Mitty. It was a relief when we finally secured a new sponsor in Burrda. In hindsight had my recommendation of the logistics firm been accepted we would have been in a far better position. They were even prepared to pay the sponsorship fee upfront.

The 2008/9 season was a relatively successful one taking into account the change in management and leadership. The club ended the season in 13th position and was seen as a work in progress after the relatively successful period under Aidy Boothroyd. The team began to play exciting football against a backdrop of uncertainty off the pitch. The games sometimes became a welcome distraction. I remember my first official visit back to Coventry City when they entertained Watford. I was in the boardroom alongside Jimmy, as he knew what this meant to me. It was a strange feeling returning back to the club that I supported and one that had played a huge part in my life. Meeting all the Coventry customers and former players and colleagues was emotional. We were all one big family. After the game, which Watford won 3-2, Jimmy asked me to show him where the dressing rooms were located. The Ricoh can be a maze at the best of times. I took Jimmy and Vince to the dressing room area, at which point Jimmy beckoned me in to the dressing room with him. The atmosphere inside, as expected, was electric and all I remember Jimmy doing was getting hold of as many worn match shirts to give away to supporters. At one point he started to look at the players' underwear, though I think he thought better of it and just kept the shirts. The players and management didn't seem to mind as Jimmy was a character after all. This once again demonstrated Jimmy's attitude to life and not having any airs and graces. I cannot imagine this happening at any other club.

The finances at Watford began to cause a strain on the board as we were into the latter stages of our parachute payments. The club still had players on Premiership wages and knew this would be an issue once the payments ended. During this period a cost-cutting exercise began as reality set in that the play-offs were now out of reach. On a personal note business was progressing and as a commercial team we were on track with most of our objectives. Much of this was made easier with the influence of Jimmy. He would always make himself available on match and non-match days. Behind the scenes very few people realised the financial issues the club was going through. Any Chairman would have faced a difficult challenge organising the fiscal issues of the club while maintaining a football squad capable of reaching the play-offs. It was evident a major cash injection was required to keep the club afloat. With Jimmy not being a majority shareholder, he was restricted to vying with the board for major decisions.

It was only a matter of time before the AGM would surface and another board upheaval would occur. The cracks off the pitch began to surface during the 2009/10 season. Malky Mackay was the new manager and began galvanising the team with his unique brand of man management. The problems off the pitch came to a head during the Christmas period. The word administration that I left at Coventry reared its ugly head once again. There were issues with Jimmy and certain members of the board about the direction of the club. There was a standoff, a game of brinkmanship that could only have one winner.

As employees of an organisation going through difficulties, it naturally affects staff, but people never seemed as concerned as the outside world think they were. In many ways it becomes a distraction, a side show, an excitement of what the next day may bring. Questions of who will take over and how it would affect the current staff could be heard in offices. You start to see people jostling for sides by hedging their bets on who will be victorious. It's amazing how the human mind works during times of adversity.

I have also been a victim of playing the diplomat and not upsetting or giving away any thoughts of support, in case you find yourself isolated with the wrong bet. It is difficult to remain impartial when opposing sides want your opinion or make comments that you may not necessarily agree with. You start thinking of the dangers of not agreeing or being seen to support the so-called opposition.

In the football industry not only are you trying to perform your day job, you also become a dab hand at politics. I genuinely believe that most people who have worked in the football industry would make great politicians. The art of remaining unbiased and yet seeming to work for all parties can be difficult but very few decide not to participate. In Jimmy and Vince's case they had supported the club by injecting several millions in loans to the club. With further funding required to stabilise the club, Jimmy and Vince wanted to become majority shareholders and operate the club as they saw fit without any obstacles. Several shareholders appeared to be reluctant to give up their shares. Inevitably this was going to the end with only one winner.

I have the utmost respect for Julian Winter, as during this difficult period he maintained absolute integrity throughout the process by not taking sides. For him it was what was best for Watford Football Club. He even argued in some cases in support of Jimmy. One incident I remember in my office, there was Julian and another senior member of staff who was persuading Julian to go against Jimmy and Vince. Julian refused to budge and said he would deal with all parties fairly, irrespective of how his position may fare from the outcome. That was the marker for how to operate in business and life.

The AGM was called in December 2009. A solution was critical to decide ownership of Watford Football Club and the long term stability of the club. The management of football never fails to shock me. There were rumours abound on the day of the AGM that Jimmy and Vince were going to resign. However, we never had any inkling that this was true from either of the brothers and thought they would find a resolution with the major shareholders. What occurred at the AGM felt like déjà vu. As in the previous season, where Graham Simpson resigned prior to the meeting, Jimmy and Vince did exactly the same. The meeting ended in two minutes and essentially we were rudderless. That evening I received several calls from Jimmy and Vince and to this day regret not having the courage to speak to them. We were all on tenterhooks and nobody was sure who we should or could speak to without being seen as disloyal or, even worse, labelled as spies in the camp. I had witnessed first-hand how people in senior positions can become paranoid in similar circumstances. It's only natural as a human to protect yourself and your family. In an ideal world you should have the freedom to speak to whoever you want to without feeling uncomfortable. Unfortunately we do not live in an ideal world and you take the necessary precautions to protect your position. The aftermath without Jimmy as Chairman was strange. I had built up a great rapport with him and had plans to expand the commercial side of the club. The only consolation was still having Julian, who now became the new CEO. I was led to believe that Lord Ashcroft pushed for Julian's appointment before committing to Watford. This spoke volumes of Julian and the way he conducted his business affairs. In all honesty there was no one who even came close to challenging Julian for the position of CEO. A new Chairman was required and there was no one better positioned to accept that role than Graham Taylor. Graham joining added a much-needed stability to Watford. In my opinion, and considering the circumstances, only someone of Graham's calibre could bring any cohesion off the pitch alongside Julian.

From a business perspective Watford enjoyed a small but loyal customer base. Over a period of three years we almost trebled the companies involved with the club through various revenue streams. Like Coventry, there were many companies who wanted to help and support us to be successful. Much of this was down to the way we managed the clients. It was refreshing to see as we were at the beginning of a recession. Over time a number of contacts became close friends and we still talk to each other to this day. At no point did we ever compromise on price, though we may have added value in some other way. Customers knew this and respected us for this. All it takes is one organisation to be given a discount and 24 hours later there is pandemonium. We are a nation who like to tell others when we have a deal. We take even more pride knowing full well your fellow colleague paid the full amount.

One of Watford's major sponsors was Peter Dean, a total gentleman and owner of the successful Happy Egg Company. There would be several times I would be around at Peter's begging for him to take a match sponsorship or sponsor the Academy. A generous, humble man, more often than not he obliged. John

Smith and his family also became good friends. John's father was the Watford Vice Chairman during the days of Elton John. We got on very well and John, like Peter, was always on hand to support us in any way he could. There were so many generous people I could literally write a book on them all.

To explain the generosity of some clients I was dealing with at Watford came to a head at the club's annual awards dinner. To make the event profitable you need several sponsors. The headline sponsor had decided not to renew on this occasion. Try as we did, we struggled to source a suitable sponsor. With time running out for printing and website designs, I decided to make one last attempt and arranged a meeting with Ken Sanker who owned a mergers and acquisitions company based in Mayfair. Ken was an affable character who always struck me as a visionary. He had also paid a significant amount of money to be allowed in the boardroom at home matches. An inquisitive businessman, over time he and I became good friends. In every club I have worked I have made it my business to get to know all the clients. Ken was also one of those characters who could not stand small talk. As we were struggling to find a sponsor, I decided to chance it with Ken. He had always said if you need help speak to me. Well I decided to take him up on the invitation. We met in Central London at one of Ken's many restaurants. After discussing all things football Ken, being the man he is, asked what he could do for me. I had been in this situation several times and was naturally eager to secure a deal. I really needed this sponsor. If we did not find one this would be the first time the club had hosted an awards dinner without a headline sponsor. This was personal. I decided to tell Ken as it was. He looked at me and just said how much. The awards sponsorships run into thousands. Expecting him to negotiate as he knew we were desperate he simply agreed. I had to check a couple of times to ensure we were on the same page. Obviously relieved but I had to know why he agreed, as Ken was not even in the country on the day of the awards.

Later on in the year when we met up again in London I asked him outright. Why did he support me and the club? You needed help and I wanted to help. That was his answer, simple and to the point. Even during the season Ken never asked for anything or expected favours in return. Meeting characters like Ken proves to me there are good people in our society and at all the clubs I have worked at I have met several like Ken. What I noticed more so with Watford was the geography of where these companies came from. Most of the companies we worked with were from all over the London area and not necessarily Watford supporters. There was not the close-knit rivalry you may find north of Watford. Companies were generally much more open to what we had to offer commercially. One of the hospitality lounges had members who supported a range of clubs such as Tottenham, West Ham and even Barnet. Much of this was also to do with the new concept I had employed to engage companies in the area to work with each other. Many clubs have still not grasped the community and business power they have at their disposal. I had simply replicated the business club we had formed at Coventry and enhanced it.

Once again, as we approached the end of the 2011 season, there was talk of new owners. I had yet to experience any stability at the club. The Chairman Graham Simpson and Chief Executive Mark Ashton had resigned within six months of me joining. A year later Jimmy and Vince resigned. Then almost 15 months later a new owner by the name of Laurence Bassini had taken over. A year after Laurence's reign there was another takeover. After the new takeover in 2012 I moved on.

Not sure why but I always end up at clubs commercially in the shit, though I would like to think I play a part in supporting clubs through difficult periods. It's a bit like Quantum Leap with the Chairman thinking thanks Raj, all sorted here, now on your bike, go and assist some other club in trouble. I just wish I could have a season of tranquillity.

After Jimmy and Vince's resignation we did have a period of calm and for a short while there was a feeling we could actually go on and progress on and off the pitch. With Graham Taylor as Chairman, Julian Winter as CEO and Malky Mackay as manager we did experience several months of normality. Though in the background you always felt things could change anytime. On the pitch, under Malky's leadership, we did flirt with promotion. The football was exciting and the club continued in its tradition of producing good academy kids for the first team. I also noticed when visiting the training ground how disciplined the players were. There was a loyal group mentality amongst the players and management and that reflected on the pitch. The fifteen months or so under Graham Taylor and Julian Winter was so smooth that it almost passed by without any issues of note. Once again I realised nothing remains the same in football for too long as eventually the club was sold to new owners.

It was also during this time when I was introduced to the legendary boxer Errol Christie by a mutual friend. We became good friends and I realised he was just about making ends meet. On several occasions Errol would mention to me he felt he was not getting any support from the industry he had given so much to. With this in mind, and to raise money for him, I decided to host a sporting dinner in his honour with the support of local Coventry businessmen and the Coventry Telegraph. This was all organised on a voluntary basis. The venue was the Standard Triumph Club where Errol first began his boxing career. It was a fabulous evening attended by many boxing fans and included former Coventry City players Cyrille Regis, Dave Bennett and Marcus Hall. It was a nostalgic evening listening to one of the greats. To the best of my knowledge this was the first and only dinner Errol ever spoke at. Errol and his son did manage to attend a Watford fixture as my guest, though somehow I don't think football really was ever his sport!

Back to the reality of life at Watford, the first time I actually met Laurence was at the Crystal Palace fixture at Selhurst Park. There were a number of us who had made the trip and Julian had invited Laurence into the boardroom as one of our guests. He introduced himself to us all and was generally quiet throughout the evening, though I did note he was becoming excited with the slim chance of Watford making the play-offs. He kept talking about the Premiership and the prospect of playing the top teams. Unfortunately we were way off the play-offs, though decided not to alert him to this incidental fact. That would have been a bad start to our first meeting. The staff simply prepared themselves for a new owner with the confidence of Julian Winter still being at the helm as CEO. That was important to all the employees, which demonstrated the respect Julian had amongst the Watford staff. The caveat to Laurence taking over the club, I later discovered, included Julian remaining as CEO. This was important for the stability of the club.

There were lighter moments when Laurence and a colleague decided to join in training with the Watford first team one morning. They both just turned up at the Colney training ground fully kitted up. Some of the players I spoke to afterwards could not believe an owner and his acquaintance had turned up to take part in training.

With time I got to know Laurence much better and

have to say he was always pleasant to myself, albeit a little interesting with his opinions. It was a difficult two to three months convincing Laurence and his team that we were the right set of employees to take them forward. One of the major blows to the club during this period was the resignation of Julian Winter. Julian had made a name for himself as a quality CEO and the only calming influence who could keep the strong personalities in check. On a personal note Julian had been a major influence on my career always encouraging me to better myself in the football industry.

After weeks of jockeying, the club finally settled down and we all moved back into our regular routine. The business continued to perform well off the pitch. At times I would wonder how all the staff at Watford remained motivated and performed to the best of their ability. We were holding our own commercially though still trying to plug the gaps in some areas which were challenging.

The new owners came in like a scene out of a Quentin Tarantino movie. There was a stream of people almost every working day. I even mistook one of Laurence's acquaintances as a major shareholder. The way this particular person wore his shades and dressed, I genuinely thought this was one of the big players in the takeover. He commanded more respect than anyone else. At one particular home match I went out of my way to introduce myself and offer a lowdown of the club. As he did not say much I thought he was assessing the club and employees. In time we realised he was Laurence's driver and probably didn't understand or care what I was talking about. I vividly remember one particular time where after a game I was introduced to a fashion designer. There was excited talk of producing a shirt that would be out of this world, different to any conventional football shirt. Great until we heard the shirt would be pink with various designs to make it stand out. This was a football club not a catwalk. I am open to new ideas but some things are just best left alone. I'm not sure why, but I never did meet the fashion designer again. Another one who came on the scene for ten minutes then suddenly disappeared. This was the theme for the first few months and as if by chance things did settle down and we became a football club once again. On the pitch Sean Dyche had replaced Malky Mackay as manager and continued to get the best out of the players. Sean had one of the lowest budgets in the league yet somehow ensured Watford continued to punch above their weight. Sean was also an approachable manager who understood the commercial constraints at the club and would do all he could to support the commercial team. Like Malky, Sean and I have stayed in touch and he always makes time for people.

UNFINISHED BUSINESS

It was during the takeover by Laurence that I was approached by a Coventry City Director, who I will refer to as Cliff, and his business associate who was responsible for running Coventry City Football Club. This continued over the coming months and after several meetings they offered me the Commercial Director's position. How this developed could have been a sketch from the Monty Python team. With Coventry struggling commercially they needed an experienced Commercial Executive who knew the city and more importantly had the experience and knowledge to turn a commercial crisis around. Prior to meeting Cliff, I was initially approached by my good friend Noel Hand, an Associate Director at the time at Coventry City. He had lobbied for my return due to the commercial revenue being in steep decline. The CEO for Coventry City at the time agreed to meet me. What I did not know was the CEO had someone else in mind and our meeting was just a formality. However the interview or informal chat was quite bizarre. The meeting took place in the Singers bar at the Ricoh Arena in earshot of anyone sat nearby. It did feel strange to have an interview for an executive position in a bar. After a while I sensed something was not quite right. The CEO kept mentioning that I was not right for the role. Criticism is hard to take at the best of times, but to tell me two minutes into our meeting without reading my CV was appalling. It became apparent he had someone else in mind as only days later he appointed a new Commercial Director who lasted one day. The CEO had forgotten to ask for references and complete his due diligence!

Eventually I was offered the Commercial Director's role and a letter of intent was emailed to me. After a few amendments I agreed. Cliff was adamant I had to hand in my notice to Watford as soon as possible, with my contract literally days away with his lawyers. I was nervous, though one of the Coventry Directors whom I had known for almost 20 years also encouraged me to do so and at times you think there needs to be an element of trust. Laurence was not too pleased at all. In some ways I felt complimented. Whenever he would see me he would make sarcastic comments about me leaving and made several attempts to convince me to stay. Coventry was my hometown and I had unfinished business to tend to. What happened next could only happen in football or as in this case Coventry City Football Club.

After handing in my notice at Watford, one of the Coventry Directors phoned to say the club wanted to make an official announcement on a particular day. I was not comfortable as I was weeks away from joining. They had asked for John Sillett, the former manager and Club President, to be part of the press call. On the same day it transpired Coventry's CEO had resigned. The club wanted to make a positive announcement and hoped the CEO leaving would not become another negative story for the club's fans to grasp. I only discovered this afterwards. The picture was taken and fortunately not released. I say fortunate as I did not want any press release until I received my official contract. Over the next few days I became a little agitated as suddenly Cliff became a forlorn figure and not contactable. Out of the blue I received an email from Cliff requesting the Coventry Chairman and I to contact each other before we proceed. How bizarre that the Chairman of Coventry was allegedly in the dark of my appointment. I believe he had no idea I was being recruited. I was now in a situation where I had handed my notice into Watford with no formal contract at Coventry. In essence I was about to become unemployed. In the coming days I spoke to certain aides at Watford and explained the situation. Once Laurence heard of my situation he offered me the Commercial Director's role immediately. I was officially employed again, with the position I wanted and had worked extremely hard for. I remember phoning and emailing Cliff with an ultimatum of receiving the contract by a certain time or I was out. The contract never materialised. I thought nothing in football would shock me; well, anything in football is possible. It's no surprise Cliff was sent overseas and never heard of again.

Moving on, I was now the first British-born Asian to become a Commercial Director of an English professional football club and I was proud of the achievement. It may have happened through the most bizarre of circumstances. Nevertheless it happened. This also coincided with me becoming nominated for an award at the inaugural Asian Football Awards ceremony to be hosted at Wembley Stadium. I was excited just to be nominated in my category. This covered a wide variety of departments. The calibre of people in all the categories was of a high standard. A few weeks prior to the event I received a call saying I had now made the shortlist and was in contention of winning my category. If I was excited to be nominated I was now ecstatic to have made the shortlist. The judges amongst others consisted of Brendan Batson (Football Association) and Arun Kang, CEO of Sporting Equals. Entitled to take a guest to the ceremony, I ensured Sharon accompanied me. I was a little cynical knowing this is an Asian event and along with timings there must be a catch somewhere. From beginning to end the ceremony was very well-organised with no expense spared. There were many well known figures out that night from the world of football which naturally adds kudos to the event.

Seated with us were the other nominees and to be honest, at this stage, I whispered to Sharon that I had no chance of winning. One of my major competitors was the Finance Director from the Football Association. The awards ceremony was on time and eventually it came to my category. It was just great to be on the shortlist and I had psyched myself up to enjoy the evening and nothing more. After listing the names on the screen one of the sponsors had to read out the winner. My name was mentioned and Sharon just looked at me as if to say you have won. I honestly thought they were reading out from third place down to the winner. My name was mentioned again and at this stage the table started congratulating me. I had just won my category! I wasn't prepared for this and had not even thought of a speech. Walking on stage and collecting the trophy was the easy bit. Next they just handed me a microphone. For a second I was stumped not sure what to say besides thanking all the relevant people, which the previous winners had already said. For a couple of minutes I mumbled along about how it is an honour to win the award and to be the first Asian Commercial Director of a club which sounded like I was pumping gas up my arse. Then I remembered my mate Andy Moss's quotes that just came out as if I had rehearsed the whole thing. What started as a disaster ended a success. Guests were applauding me for the last part of the speech and how it resonated with them. It was all made up and I cannot even remember exactly what I said. I took the plaudits and enjoyed the moment. To some, winning awards means very little. To me it was an achievement of being recognised in my industry. The Asian Awards were also to recognise the efforts of Asians in football and sent a positive message to Asians outside the industry that there are opportunities and possibilities in the game. It was important to have key figures such as the CEO of the Football Association David Bernstein in attendance, who in my opinion was an excellent ambassador for the F.A. and easily accessible.

As Commercial Director it was quite a smooth

transition from directing the sales team to now also leading the retail and ticketing operations. I genuinely believed I could make a success of what was required from me. I also discovered your peers treat you the way you hold and see yourself. Even during difficult times it is incredible how we find a way to deal with challenging situations.

The immediate concerns were finding another new shirt sponsor, halting the decline of season tickets and securing a new shirt manufacturer all in the space of a few months. In football there are no half measures; it's all or nothing such is the pressure cooker you are dealing with.

Paul Fletcher had always said to me your next shirt sponsor is in the stand. How true his words were. As mentioned previously I knew Peter Dean, the owner of the Happy Egg Company. He always acted with class and made time for people. He was one of those people you could go to if you needed support to fill the last sponsorship category or something similar. However this was a shirt sponsorship and we were looking for a six figure sum. The initial contact with Peter was lukewarm. Out of courtesy he asked me to send a proposal and nothing really materialised. For some unknown reason I had this feeling something good will come. It was a visceral emotion that's hard to quantify as I had nothing to go on. It all happened at the Watford player of the year event. Last minute I was asked to sit with Peter as a way of respecting his support for the club. We spoke about many things that evening but never touched on the shirt sponsorship. At the end of the evening Peter simply turned around to me and said you're not yourself what's the issue. I just mentioned that the shirt sponsorship was essentially my responsibility and I was struggling to gain interest. If the board could not generate any interest what chance did I have? He looked at me and said I will do it.

That comment threw me completely and whilst I knew what had been said I deliberately refrained from asking Peter to repeat himself. I just wanted to hold those words in the palm of my hands for as long as possible. I just wanted to cherish a few moments to myself. Then reality set in and I had to reconfirm what I thought Peter had just said. Well second time around he said it again and this time I knew I had just secured our new shirt sponsor.

The sponsorship itself was unique in that my colleague Andrea Viglieno and I had designed the logo with a QR code so supporters across the UK and even the world could go onto the website of Happy Egg and Watford Football Club using their smart phones. Simple yet revolutionary, Watford Football Club was supposed to be the first club in the world to feature a QR code as part of the shirt sponsorship. I say supposedly because in due course change was about to occur that would impact me hugely. The renowned and respected F.C. Business magazine featured the article with the QR code and were eulogising about a small provincial club making positive strides to offer a genuine ROI to shirt partners. The relief of securing a new shirt sponsor was short-lived. It was a distressed sale and Peter always made it clear he had no qualms of moving to one side if another party came to the table, which was eventually the case.

Prior to the new takeover you could sense the despondency amongst the staff. The tension started to build in the offices, irrespective of the assurances we were getting from some members of the board. Talk of administration and possible redundancies surfaced once more, though this time there was a real feeling something was not quite right. During this particular period, and as reported in the local paper, Laurence made one of his visits to the office. On this occasion he wanted the cash from the club safe. The Head of Finance was under strict instructions not to release any money from the safe. But refusing to give Laurence the money merely angered him. This was an embarrassing situation, with all the office staff watching in disbelief. In some respects I felt sorry for him. Eventually, after calling the police and publicly sacking the employee in question, he finally got hold of the small amount of cash in the safe. He actually verbally sacked two members of staff that afternoon. They had a few weeks off at home and made their appearance once the new takeover from Laurence was complete. From an unbiased perspective, Laurence as owner did have the right to the monies as it was still his club. Taking out the ethics and morals, it was still his club. However, in hindsight it was unfair to put the finance person in such a difficult position especially as she was only carrying out instructions given to her by a particular member of the board.

Each day was about survival. The management meetings I attended were a formality and a talking shop of what was happening at the club. We had no power or authority to make important decisions. Amidst all the issues and ongoing problems, respect must go to all the staff for holding together a club in transition. I tried to maintain a positive attitude and allowed managers from the ticket office, retail and commercial departments to have the autonomy to make decisions and continue the progress of recent months. We halted the season ticket demise and for the first time in five seasons sold more season tickets than the previous season. Retail was looking healthy even though they were operating out of a hut.

Talk about an imminent takeover was rife. I remember speaking to prospective buyers a few months earlier and explaining the commercial aspects of the club and the endless opportunities we could tap into given the resources. We needed a solution and we needed a buyer very soon. Whilst rumours were rife of whom the new owners would be, reality set in when it was announced we had agreed a deal with an Italian consortium. The day of the actual takeover was in July 2012. Unfortunately, as with most takeovers, there was a restructuring and I found myself seeking new opportunities. Watford, the club that changed me and gave me one of the most enjoyable experiences in football, was over. I was now embarking upon a new journey. During my time at Watford I had the pleasure of working with Graham Taylor who, as Chairman, was always available to speak to. He made time for the staff and was a true professional during the challenging times at the club. This for me sums up his character.

Looking back at my time at Watford, I never had a settled season in my four years there and yet we still delivered challenging budgets which I attribute to the positive attitude of the commercial team. One of my colleagues, former Watford player Neil Price, can best be described as a maverick but never let me down. If any of our customers were unsure of renewing their memberships I would send Neil to speak to them. Most often they would sign up for another season. Neil proved the value former players can have for their respective clubs. It was never plain sailing – we made mistakes but that's life and you have to accept the rough with the smooth and move on. Overall I would say my time at Watford was exciting, challenging, bordering on complete madness; but extremely enjoyable.

This was the first time in 18 years that I decided to have a brief hiatus from working in the football industry. A month to reflect on the past, what I had achieved, what I could have done better and to enjoy the simple things in life. It felt like a revelation waking up in the morning and not feeling any pressure. For the first time in a long while I was happy and enjoying life. It's amazing how the simple things in life are the most enjoyable. I actually felt liberated from the stresses of life. No more pressures of the modern football world. I fell into a career in football, though for now I was extremely content.

After several weeks I decided to contact some of my closest friends and their support was overwhelming. What really struck me was the kindness of one particular customer from Watford called Terry Batchelor. He managed to get hold of my mobile from the club and called me to offer money if I needed it. Just the thought made me realise the kindness that exists in our society. I didn't need the money but to have a pensioner call to offer me £500 was mind-blowing. Terry called again stating I only had to pay him back as and when I had the money. I was absolutely fine but he was not aware of my situation. His act of kindness restored my faith in humanity once again.

When a person is at their peak psychologically you feel you can take on the world. There are no barriers to what you can aspire to. The mental blocks no longer exist. Your thoughts are constantly interchanging with new ideas and models of excellence that can enhance you spiritually. Post-Watford I had lost my drive and was in danger of losing my way altogether. I began to question my own ability. You lose focus on what you have achieved and concentrate on proverbial weaknesses. The mind goes into overdrive and it can potentially become a dangerous situation especially when you begin analysing. No matter how hard I tried to convince myself that I would move on to better things I just could not be motivated.

It was then a friend called, which was my saving grace and a major lesson in life. You are never alone and when times are difficult and you can see no way out, speak up.

Peter Marsden, who at the time was the Chairman of Accrington Stanley Football Club, had been trying to contact me when he realised I was no longer at Watford

Football Club. He wanted to utilise my knowledge and experience in the interim to assist the Commercial Manager at Accrington Stanley. Curiosity and the need to be proactive got the better of me and I agreed to help. This was a temporary measure while I decided on my next journey.

PIT STOP TO ACCRINGTON STANLEY

I had no idea what to expect at Accrington. On my first day I was immediately introduced to Paul Cook, the manager at the time. We hit it off immediately and spoke at length about our experiences in football. However, when enquiring about his opinion of football in the lower leagues I was taken aback. Having worked in the Premiership and the Championship, you generally take many things for granted, even basic necessities such as having an office and a desk to work from.

The lounge I was sat in talking to the manager was the office that converted to a match day lounge for visiting Directors. This was the hub of the club on non-match days, where most of the staff including Academy coaches worked from. There were no desks so you had to improvise when trying to use your laptop! This was also where I met Simon Cooper, who can best be described as lightyears ahead when it comes to coaching budding footballers. It was Simon who persuaded me to follow one of my ambitions to begin writing about my experiences in life and football. There was a boardroom next door which also doubled up as an office. This was the reality of a lower league club, albeit a famous one. As mentioned earlier, I got chatting to Paul on my first day and to hear a manager say that the average weekly wage of his players was in the low hundreds completely stifled me. I expected more but this was the reality at a small club who were more than punching above their weight. Paul came across as a clever coach who made a positive impression the first moment you met him. We immediately started talking shop about players, the club and what he was determined to achieve with the set of players at his disposal. The key here was Accrington had the lowest playing budget in the league and yet were almost in touching distance of the play-offs. They did lose their way as the season progressed, but for me this was due to the lack of resources as opposed to the determination of the playing staff. I was not used to a manager sitting having coffee with me discussing his tactics and issues with football. It was refreshing though somewhat surreal.

The Kit Manager, Naz Ali, was a young aspiring law graduate who was working on a voluntary basis. His situation was such that the first team would raise a kitty after every match to help Naz out. Here was a lad that was as dedicated as anyone at the club working for nothing. Yet he would show great pride in ensuring all the kits were washed on time and the players had their training gear ready each morning. Naz was operating out of what can only be described as an old decrepit shed. He had my full respect and we have remained friends ever since. The dressing rooms were portable cabins and were just about fit for purpose. Yet the players never complained and just got on with the job in hand. What also struck me was the players never had the so called big brand new cars. Some of the players I spoke to were just about surviving on a weekly basis. The highest earner was allegedly on only £800 per week. Accrington was a stepping stone to a bigger club with a much more generous salary. This totally blew the myth I had of what professional players were earning. Now this was a family and the players were no prima donnas. They were dedicated professionals who wanted to make a career out of football. I received more respect from the Accrington lads than some players at other clubs I had worked at. From top to bottom I was made very welcome. Tony Allen, the club's Commercial Manager, was a real gentleman and man of great integrity and honesty. His attitude to work and life was to give his best at all times, even in the face of criticism. Tony had been in football for many years working as a company secretary. Now he was at Accrington in a commercial role. Admittedly I was unsure of his skill set commercially but felt he deserved a chance. Over time Tony more than proved he was capable but, like most Commercial Managers at lower league clubs, they have very little support or resource and are expected to generate revenue whilst acting as a Retail Assistant, emptying the bins and driving the academy kids to and from home every day!

The short time I spent at Accrington was enjoyable and an eye opener. I helped Tony add focus to the commercial department and advised members of the board where they needed to deliver resources. Commercially Accrington had the potential to generate much more revenue than they were currently achieving. For me it was a question of resources and structure. The Company Secretary, for instance, doubled up as the maintenance man and safety officer on match days. On non match days he would be acting as Ticket Office Manager one minute and Shop Assistant the next. This was the reality of clubs at the lower echelons of the league. The club quite frankly needed re-organising from top to bottom. To the outside world the media has created a false image for supporters whereby they believe their club is operating like a normal business. Why should they think any different when you have successful business people represented on the Board of Directors? The issue is with resources. The same people on the board probably have all the key elements in their own business to make it a success. From sales and marketing to fully qualified accountants and IT experts their own businesses are probably solid. What I was experiencing in most clubs in the lower leagues was the desire to make cuts in areas that generate revenue. Rather than cut sales, people or personnel that are conducive to generating revenue, it makes more sense to bring in new recruits. It's reverse psychology but it works. I have seen this on so many occasions and Paul Fletcher proved the point at Coventry. Cutting off the one department that brings in revenue is suicidal.

Business really is not that difficult if you have the right blend of people who are prepared to push the barriers. Whatever the outcome, you can only gain from the experience. Not to take risks is safe. However, to remain in a state of inertia is too risky. The club needed someone to operate with complete autonomy and a workable budget to make the necessary changes. Accrington has the potential to become a progressive professional football club. The employees are delivering multiple roles and need support and resources to operate effectively. Accrington punched above its weight and respect has to be given to the Chairman, the Board of Directors and the employees for keeping it functioning on extremely limited resources.

On one particular occasion the Chairman suggested I become the new Commercial Director and effectively work with the current Managing Director to re-organise the club. At this stage in my career it did not appeal to me. As I said before, there was no real commercial structure and with the current set up I could not visualise change. There needed to be a complete change of ownership and direction if Accrington was to progress. The club needed a major overhaul and serious investment to just compete on and off the pitch. In the football world most clubs are simply surviving on a day to day basis and Accrington was no different. I developed a fondness for the club and helped where I could. Peter and the board supported the club and did all they could for no personal gain. They needed some luck and a wealthy investor.

After a short break I began to really use my networks to find a suitable position in football. I decided to stay in the game as I had so much to offer and new ideas to pursue. Over a two year period the commercial income at Watford had seen a major increase from the previous season's and I knew I could replicate this model elsewhere. I just needed another opportunity. I set myself a goal of securing a suitable position within four weeks. Each night I would write a timetable for the next day. I was completely focussed. The short period at Accrington had done wonders for my-self esteem. Andy Ward, who was a former colleague of mine, was now at Southampton F.C. I mentioned to him I was looking for a commercial role and, like everyone else, he said he would keep me posted if anything transpired. Another contact of mine, Ryan McKnight, the former editor of F.C Business, stated he was about to be offered a major role and would want me to join him as his Commercial Director. This all sounded promising. To stay disciplined and focussed I joined a local gym in East Street, Coventry, near to the old Highfield Road stadium. A friend of mine could see I needed an outlet so took me over to the Lions Gym one morning. It was a no-frills gym located in a small industrial estate. Not sure what to expect I was pleasantly surprised with the positive vibe I felt from the place. The best way to describe it is to think of the gym in the Rocky films where Stallone trained. It's clean but has a raw edge to the place. The people attending were from all walks of life, different races, backgrounds and culture, yet in that place everyone is equal. The customers were not pretentious or judgemental.

In the Lions Gym you are all one community fighting for the same cause. How coincidental for the gym to be situated next door to a gospel church. The Lord surely does move in mysterious ways. The Lions Gym gave me a purpose. I could think while getting fit. Just attending two to three times per week removed so much of the pressure. It clears your head and energises you to be productive for the rest of the day.

The gym itself has this aura about it. It brought me back to my working class roots. At those times as a young adult you have all these dreams and aspirations. Anything is possible in life. This is exactly what the gym did and still does for me. It's a mechanism that encourages me to remember what I am here for. In Watford I would attend the local gym that had all the facilities you could dream of. Yet I enjoyed this gym the least. That's the point in life; you can have everything you ever dreamed of but don't forget the fundamental ingredients that got you there in the first place. Places like the Lions Gym brought me back to my dreams. You just need to find what works for you.

Reflecting on my time at Coventry and Watford, I had many days of insecurity, doubts and fears. I discovered ways of turning those emotions into positives that worked for me as opposed to against me. In life and society there will always be people preventing you from progressing. This can be due to jealousy, envy or a reflection of their lives, not necessarily for ulterior motives. Trying to move beyond those barriers is difficult and this is where a person must be strong and emotionally persistent to move forward. We all have different circumstances and some find themselves in a complete rut they just cannot find a way out of. Just surviving day to day is a reality for many. I should know – I have experienced many situations where you feel you are constantly hitting a brick wall. There are no easy solutions, though I genuinely believe that with the right mentors and support mechanism we all have the ability to progress and achieve our dreams. There are good people out there in society who want to help and most of the time will do so because that gives them a sense of satisfaction. Nothing is impossible and we should have a platform where adults from all walks of life have the opportunity to work with successful mentors. These people can give a real insight into the way they think, act and perceive their life.

Young adults need to be influenced by people that have lived, breathed and overcome adversity. I have personally thought about setting up a foundation supporting British kids, utilising the skills of business professionals and sports athletes. Each city would have its own mentors who are dedicated to helping a generation find their way in life. It's charity work which will be hugely rewarding. My desire to help is due to so many people over the years supporting me in my time of need. Negative emotions do not discriminate and can affect any person, irrespective of their status. If you can learn to train your emotions you are almost in control of your own destiny.

I have also witnessed intelligent young people lose their way and become a burden to themselves and their families. Just one chance, meeting the right person, encouragement and support could make all the difference to one's life. It's not about blaming people around you or your environment – that's an excuse. For me it's having the right support and people who have overcome adversity to give you the correct advice. Kids from disadvantaged backgrounds have a tougher life and lower expectations but they also have the same aspirations and dreams as kids from the other side of the spectrum. There is a tipping point in every child or adult's life where one turn can either be beneficial or detrimental. For me, if we can capture a kid before they fall, we are giving them the biggest gift of all – faith. This responsibility should not be entirely on the shoulders of teachers or social workers or parents. We as one have the responsibility.

I know of many successful people in their industry

who would be pleased to offer their time. Where do they start or go to? I know of schemes to help kids but for me they are few and far between. This is not a criticism of charities or pressure groups. It's an observation of our so-called politics. They all focus on the macro level of society without understanding the real issues locally. I have lived all over the UK and I am yet to meet my local councillor. If we really want change then we need to challenge our own thought processes.

THE MIGHTY GLASGOW RANGERS

Within four weeks I had a call from Andy Ward asking if I would be willing to travel to Scotland. The mighty Glasgow Rangers had a senior commercial position available. Immediately, without thinking, I said yes – after all, this was one of the biggest clubs in the world. At the same time Ryan Mcknight called me to say he has secured a CEO position at Stockport County and would I accompany him to Manchester to meet one of the investors, as he had put me forward for the Commercial Director's position. A few days later I received an email from the Group Commercial Director at the F.A., who was asked by David Bernstein, the F.A. Chairman, to see me. It was purely an exploratory meeting. Since my Coventry days I realised to get anywhere in life you need to speak to the decision maker. As with Bryan Richardson, I always attempted to speak to someone who could make the ultimate decisions. It appears they hardly ever receive letters or calls as people tend to only go through the conventional channels.

My objectives were on target and I just knew I was onto something really good. Within the space of a week I was meeting and speaking to three organisations. I travelled to Stockport with Ryan as he was about to be unveiled on Sky Sports as the youngest male CEO of a professional football club in the UK. I had been to Edgeley Park before when Coventry played Stockport County, their first match in the Championship, so had an idea of the set up there. While Ryan was going through the motions with the media team I spent some time with one of the investors. I was impressed with the investor, who had a real understanding of business and came across in a very honest way. This was unusual in football.

However we hit it off from the start. The investor hinted they were going to offer me the Commercial Director's position. It was literally a formality once Ryan had been appointed.

During the same period I spoke to Irene Munro, the Marketing Director for Glasgow Rangers. I briefly explained what I could bring to the table and about my invaluable experience and knowledge in dealing with clubs that were struggling commercially. To know how to generate revenue during difficult times appealed to Rangers. Irene wasted no time in inviting me up to Glasgow. Suddenly I had three potential opportunities with Rangers, Stockport and the F.A.

I had kept Ryan informed of the meetings I had with Rangers and the F.A. While I was in a very strong position, Ryan was keen to get me on board as soon as possible. A very good offer was emailed a couple of days before I was to travel up to Scotland with a promise of a good commission structure. Ryan and the investor had been fair in their offer as Stockport were now plying their trade in the conference league. I had one concrete offer, but it was Glasgow Rangers that really excited me.

I remember the morning I was to travel to Glasgow. There had been a heavy snowfall and I was concerned of any delays. I was a mixture of nerves, anticipation and, in some ways, excitement to travel to Glasgow. In fact I had never been to Scotland, never mind Glasgow. This was like a mini holiday. At last I was to visit the famous Ibrox Stadium. The beginning of the journey was not exactly a great start. The train was delayed and as I was catching a connecting train at Birmingham, it was touch and go. Well, I missed the Birmingham connection and had to wait another half hour before catching the train to Glasgow. There was one more stop at Carlisle but I was already late and there was nothing I could do about the situation.

On arriving at Central Station in Glasgow the sun was shining and I felt something good would come of the day. I caught a taxi to Ibrox Stadium and was impressed with the driver, who explained all there was to know about Rangers in record time. I wasn't sure of his allegiances but at one point he thought I was an investor and started telling me what I needed to do to make the club more profitable. He certainly set the scene for the future. Travelling to Ibrox was a fifteen minute drive and in that time I tried to view as much of Glasgow as I could. We drove by the River Clyde and over the Squinty Bridge. Impressed by the architecture and tenement flats we suddenly came across the Loudon Bar which I remembered from a previous TV documentary. When we eventually arrived at Ibrox, I was in awe of the famous stadium. Watching it on TV and then seeing it in the flesh is a completely different feeling. Ibrox Stadium had this imperious feel about it, hard to put into words, though anyone who has seen the stadium will know exactly what I am talking about. This huge listed building stood right in front of me and I was about to be interviewed for a major role at Rangers Football Club. This was mine for the taking, I just knew it.

I made my way round to the Argyle Reception. The reception was tired but the pictures of the Rangers Legends brought the place to life. Players who graced Ibrox and were now watching over you included Gazza, McCoist, Gough, Goram, Hateley. This was more than just a football club, this was an institution. The heritage, tradition and culture of Rangers could be felt just standing in the reception area. Opposite the reception area were huge billboard posters with all things Rangers, such as hospitality and football kits for sale. Tracy, the receptionist, was a bubbly, larger than life character and made you feel comfortable the moment you entered reception. Those first impressions were important and set the scene for my interview.

Irene came to greet me herself and we made our way up to her office on the first floor. Admittedly the stairs and walls made me feel cold – it was like walking up terraces from the 70s. However, once you get to the main office area it does improve, though not by much. What did strike me was the tired feel of the offices, which were in need of some major refurbishment. To me this was a throwback to the 80s and in some way I related to the décor and feel of the place, as this was the Rangers I knew and admired. It also reminded me of the Highfield Road offices. It's interesting when you attend interviews how people suddenly change and become someone else rather than be themselves. I was conscious of staying true to myself and to remain confident at all times. Time and time again I remembered to listen and only speak when you need to. Interrupting when someone is halfway through their conversation is one way of going home early. I do have a bad habit due to my energy to interrupt just so I don't lose my train of thought.

Irene herself was a very smart lady in her early forties. She certainly did not look like the person I envisaged on the phone. I was not sure why but in my mind I envisaged Irene as a much older and tougher personality. To the contrary Irene was a dynamic go-getter who managed many departments. She was charming, though you knew get on the wrong side of her and you were asking for trouble.

I had my laptop ready with a strategy of how I was going to turn around the commercial fortunes of Rangers. The presentation took around 40-45 minutes and as I was going through my presentation I was becoming more and more confident. I had travelled over five hours to get here and I was not going home without leaving a lasting impression. More importantly, I wanted Irene to offer me the position. After my presentation and discussing Rangers in general Irene got straight to the point. "I want to offer you the job" and gave me a starting figure. Originally when I spoke to Irene the salary was much lower than what I was earning at Watford. Rather than turn the position down, I thought why not show them what I am capable of and how much more revenue I can generate for the club. For a small compromise I would be generating significantly more revenue that would compensate for my increase. Irene and I eventually agreed on a figure, shook hands and the deal was complete. If I learned a valuable lesson that morning it was how to negotiate a deal without undervaluing yourself. Irene did not give me time to think she agreed the deal and said "right, the job's yours, when can you start?" I was left with no alternative but to accept and, being a man of my word, I had just joined Rangers Football Club with no time to enjoy the opportunity.

In record time I had met the Rangers Marketing Manager, who was as shocked as me in the speed of my appointment. Irene and I made our way up to the second floor where one of the club Directors was located. Immediately he started to discuss the shirt sponsorship and how it was yet to be signed. *Not again,* I thought; no matter which club I speak to they all need a shirt sponsor when I turn up. Can I not join a club where the shirt is sponsored with three to four years to go before expiring, allowing me to focus on developing the commercial aspects of the department? Fortunately the shirt sponsorship was completed by the time I started. That was a relief for now. I say for now, as the deal was only for one season and yes, you have guessed it, I had seven months to find a new one unless Tennants renewed. As fate would have it, Tennants decided not to renew just before Christmas, allowing me only three months to find a new sponsor.

Throughout the club I was welcomed by some of the kindest, most dedicated people I had ever met in the industry. Rangers were their life and they certainly let you know in no uncertain terms what this club meant to them and the supporters. From the supporters to the corporate members I was welcomed with open arms. At my first ever home fixture one of the long-serving stewards said now you have joined the Rangers, you will always be a Ranger. Not until I left the club did those words mean anything to me. Rangers overtakes your life and in turn you become a part of the club. It becomes your family.

After meeting various people at the club I was given a full tour of the facilities. Entering the stadium was incredible. Just walking alongside the pitch gave you a sense of pride. At one point I just had to stop and stare at the Main Stand, where the words Glasgow Rangers looked back at me. *This is what dreams are made of,* I thought to myself. Walking through the tunnel is mesmerising, with such a grand area littered with the history of the club. The marble pillars and flooring was something I had never seen before in a tunnel area. The honours and achievements of the club adorned the walls, which must add to the nerves of the away team before they even set foot on the pitch. This was, after all, a five-star European stadium and I had just signed up to work here. That bit never really crossed my mind as I walked into the dressing rooms. The home dressing room was very spacious. It had this powerful aura about it. What immediately struck me were two pictures of the Queen. This must be the only football club on earth with two pictures of the Queen in a dressing room! It was also interesting to see the old hooks on dressing room walls for players to hang up their football kits. The hooks were from a bygone era as they were constructed to hold bowler hats. Being a listed building many of the original features remained and you could just feel and smell the history and heritage. Next we made our way to the reception area. Now this was something special. Marble floor and an opulent staircase, no expense spared by Archibald Leitch, the architect who also built the Queen Mary. There was a traditional look and feel about the place. At the top of the stairs was a huge wooden Hall of Fame board depicting the many greats who graced Ibrox. Reading the names of the players reinforced the stature of this great club.

The Blue Room, where the Directors congregated on match days, was totally different with a mixture of tradition and heritage and modernity thrown in for good measure. The architecture again was something special and unique.

The club as a whole was graced with culture, heritage and tradition. There were so many facilities to digest. The Players' Lounge was better than most dining areas I had seen. The Chairman's lounge was like something out of the Ritz. There was something for all clients and budgets. Commercially, this was going to be a challenge. Then again I was used to challenges by now and I guess why Rangers opted for my services.

After the tour and meeting several of my new colleagues, I made my way back to Central Station and that's when it hit me. In the back of the taxi, my mind was in overdrive, excited and full of thoughts. I had just agreed to join one of the biggest clubs in the world. This alone meant so much to me after years of working my ass off. The only problem was that I had not discussed this with Sharon and the family. I had just agreed on instinct. In my defence I did go with a plan and when this was agreed I just thought, *go for it*. It's not as if I was purchasing curtains without consulting my wife. That can cause havoc in any family. No, I had just agreed to join a club with a five and a half hour drive time, without even a courtesy conversation. The ideal outcome would be for me to be offered the position and then go away and come back two to three days later. To Irene's credit, she obviously had seen someone who had the experience and knowledge to do a job at Rangers in their current predicament. Irene was ruthless – it was a case of do you want the job or not. I started to play mind games. If I say I want to think about the offered position, does that appear negative or not interested? Surely not. I had just travelled to another country for an interview at the crack of dawn. I was not here to waste anyone's time. My mind was racing. This was an opportunity I had been waiting for. All those years saying I was good enough to work at any of the big clubs I just needed a chance. Here was my chance. I finally agreed. This was the famous Glasgow Rangers Football Club, a sporting institution, and this is where the next chapter of my life's journey would begin.

Arriving back in Coventry felt like an age. Once home, I tried to explain the day in a nutshell. "Have they offered you a position?" immediately asked Sharon. I tried to weave my way around the subject by discussing the day and how the train journey was long and arduous. I was looking for sympathy for my journey and got none. That evening I calmly explained that I had been offered a senior position at the club and that I had accepted. "What's the salary and what about the F.A. on Monday? You still have to meet them," replied Sharon. "What if they offer you a position that's too good to turn down?" I should have been a proud man who had just travelled hundreds of miles to look after his family and here I was at home getting the third degree from my wife. In her defence, she was right. However, sometimes in difficult circumstances you have to make difficult decisions and as the famous adage goes, time kills all deals. I had secured a position, the family would be looked after, so what was the issue? The issue was simple. I had just accepted a job hundreds of miles away. I was to start in two weeks time with no accommodation or a courteous discussion with the wife. The responsibility of looking after our children and running the household was going to fall on Sharon as I would only return at weekends every other week. Deep down I made a decision based on looking after my family and enhancing my career opportunities. I was not a twenty-something looking for a good time. I was approaching my forties and was focussed on giving my family everything I possibly could. My childhood is what drives me on and, from a personal perspective, to continuously challenge myself. My goals and objectives would not change. This would play a huge part in supporting the bigger picture and plans I had written down about how I visualised my future.

I travelled to Glasgow on Sunday 10 February 2013, a day before Sharon's birthday. I seem to be making a habit of either forgetting her birthday or having to be elsewhere. I will never forget the moment I returned home from Watford one evening. Walking through the door Simran my oldest daughter came running up to me shouting I was in deep trouble with Sharon. I just smiled thinking it must be something trivial. The smile was wiped off my face when I sat down in the living room and all I could see were birthday cards. This was the mother of all birthdays. I had only forgotten her 40th! In quick time I tried to make amends by stating I had a special present lined up. I was planning to take her to Goa, India and wanted it to be a surprise. She never bought my excuse and we are yet to travel to Goa, though the intention is still there. For the record I have never forgotten her birthday since!

It was a cold, snowbound day again. With more snow forecast, I decided to leave at lunchtime. This was an exciting journey and strangely I felt like a student once again about to embark on a new career path. The journey to Glasgow took over five hours. This was also my second visit to Scotland, though my first by car. For some reason I was excited at the prospect of travelling by car. I was like a kid about to embark on an adventure. Driving by towns and cities I had only previously seen on a map helped pass the time. I had never been as far as Carlisle. Technically I was in a different country and that itself made me feel like a seasoned traveller. In truth I was only a few hours from home, but why spoil the moment.

While driving through Scotland I could not help but admire the scenery. The hills and countryside dominated the landscape. I was passing towns and cities that I had only seen on the Final Score on a Saturday afternoon. This may seem weird but as a football fan driving past such towns gives me incredible joy similar to train enthusiasts. I am proud to say I am a football town anorak. I just enjoy going to different towns and cities and viewing their football stadiums. I have been in numerous arguments with Sharon when travelling to a particular destination and then randomly stopping off at a nearby town just to see their football stadium. Scotland had this appeal; it was new to me and I wanted to enjoy the place. The only difference compared to England is the fact it was colder, darker and seemed to rain every day. Other than those minor irritants I loved the place. To begin with I was staying at the Holiday Inn in Hamilton, which was a 15 minute drive from Ibrox.

After a restless night I made my way to Ibrox, leaving in good time to ensure I arrived early. Not knowing where to park I only ended up driving through the Ibrox car park exit gate and nearly crashed into an oncoming car. Luckily no one spotted me. There were no home comforts that I took for granted, just me and my suitcase. Reality finally hit home. Yet this was the easy bit. The next two years at Glasgow Rangers Football Club were going to be the most powerful emotional and physical rollercoaster I had ever experienced in my life. I had not realised what I had let myself into. The people of Glasgow, the city and the football club became a major part of my life and one which I will never forget. I love the people, the city and the club. They were all so good to me and took me in as one of their own. We were one huge family until my southern counterparts decided to change the club's landscape, and not necessarily for the right reasons.

ONLY IN GLASGOW

The first few days at Rangers involved getting accustomed to my colleagues and understanding the commercial areas of the club. Irene was very helpful and guided me during my first few weeks. I distinctly remember one of my colleagues giving me the dos and don'ts on working at Rangers Football Club. Do not tell the taxi driver where you work; do not wear your uniform after a match day if you intend to go out at night and do not wear the colours or a Rangers scarf outside of Ibrox. I honestly thought this was a wind-up and I simply dismissed the advice. The smiles disappeared when I realised they were deadly serious. I have grown up with people of different faiths and the thought of religion never crossed my mind when socialising or working with these people. This though felt like Belfast with a lid on it and to stay hassle-free I just had to follow the simple rules. In hindsight I should have taken the advice seriously, as I experienced some hairy moments which nearly ended in disaster. After one particular match I had arranged to meet some friends for a drink in Glasgow town centre. As I was running late I decided to just go in my Rangers uniform. What actually gives the uniform away is the red white and blue tie, which is acutely distinctive and easily recognisable to the football supporter in Glasgow. Due to the media intensity both the Rangers and Celtic club uniforms are easily recognisable even to the non-ardent supporter. With my attire I was leaving myself open to becoming a target. Upon leaving one of the bars after a couple of drinks a friend and I decided to make our way to the 29 Club, which was owned by a very well known and respected Rangers supporter. He had given me a membership card shortly after I joined Rangers. The place was quality with both lively and quiet areas to drink from. This is one place in Glasgow you would not have any trouble. On the way a couple of young, well-dressed lads suddenly stopped to ask me for the time. Not thinking anything untoward, I gave them the time and then they started to ask questions as to where I was from and what I was doing in Glasgow. It was all friendly banter at first and I thought nothing of it. My friend kept nudging me to leave but these lads just seemed like harmless, friendly Glaswegians. Suddenly out of the blue one of the lads started to become aggressive, making offensive references to Rangers Football Club. What made it worse was, as they became more and more aggressive, I failed to understand what they were actually saying. Their accents were becoming stronger, and I was struggling to make out the conversation, which made them even more aggressive. My friend, who is from Glasgow, naturally understood the lads and appeared more nervous than me. From nowhere one of the lads pulled out a bottle and smashed it against the wall. At this point I was in fear of the consequences. Trying to calm things down all I could understand is them calling me a dirty Hun. *What the fuck is a Hun*, I kept thinking to myself? The only time I have ever been called Hun was from my wife as a term of endearment. There was certainly no love in the air tonight! Fortunately there were a group of drinkers nearby who had heard the commotion and decided to find out what was going on. This is Glasgow, after all; it is everyone's business to know what's going on. *This is it*, I thought, *me and my mate were about to get battered by Glasgow's finest*. How do I explain this to the club, if I ever live to tell the story! The Almighty must have been watching because the group of lads that came over were all Rangers supporters and, realising I worked for the club, quickly stepped in. After a few words were exchanged the two aggressors left in a hurry, to the point they were almost running away. Not sure what was said but it did the trick. All this trouble because I had a Rangers tie and uniform on. On another occasion after a game Rangers had lost, I decided to do some food shopping before driving back to my flat. My shopping was easy. It was a case of which microwave meal took my fancy? After a while I started to notice an older gentleman following me wherever I was walking. He was in my personal space so to speak. Turning around to confront him I noticed he was one of the employees. He simply stood directly in front of me and started to laugh sarcastically. Not wanting to cause any commotion, even though I was the customer, I continued ignoring him. The idiot kept following me and began making silly high-pitched noises to grab my attention. He did grab my attention as well as all the other shoppers close by. He just kept laughing at me because Rangers had lost and he really didn't care of the consequences. I felt more like the perpetrator and he was the victim just because I had my Rangers uniform on. As I walked on trying to ignore this maniac he started to sing to me, which I realised were not in favour of Rangers. This was a man who did not look any younger than eighty years of age and appeared to be taking great pleasure in giving me shit in a supermarket and nobody seemed to care. Even his co-workers just looked on, probably too shocked to intervene. I only wanted a microwave meal and here I was getting all this grief for wearing a Rangers uniform. This was a supermarket, not the away end of a rival football club! Even as I walked to my car I could see him in the shop window gesturing to me. Here was an old man who should be enjoying the fruits of his life taking great pleasure in giving me the V sign simply because I was working for Rangers Football Club! I was convinced he had escaped the local psychiatric unit. To make matters worse, that evening the microwave decided to play up. After several minutes I heard a huge bang; the curry had only just gone and exploded inside the microwave, making an awful mess for me to clear up. This just about summed up my whole day. Needless to say I never wore my uniform out in Glasgow again!

Talking about match days, I remember my first home game at Ibrox and one I will never forget. Rangers were playing East Stirling. With the greatest respect this was a far cry from the SPL days against stronger opposition. However on the day there were 50,000 supporters packed into Ibrox. The atmosphere was electric and this for a League 3 game! As the teams walked out to the Penny Arcade anthem I knew I was lucky to be at such a special club. Even though Rangers won the game 3-1 I just remember being mesmerised by the supporters that sang and jumped throughout the game to the famous bouncy bouncy chant. Another surprise in store which I had no idea of was when the supporters began singing God Save the Queen in the 89th minute. This was a ritual at every home game. If I was in awe of the noise against East Stirling what would the atmosphere be like against Celtic!

Business-wise the commercial targets had been set, though Irene wanted to increase the income. I had after all promised her I was the saving grace that Rangers needed during their time of need. After much deliberation our commercial budgets were prepared and they were extremely challenging. I always believed in my ability and now was the time to prove my worth once again. At Rangers you always feel under the spotlight and that's just with your peers. Pressure though brings the best out of me; the creative juices start flowing with the belief and confidence that anything is achievable in life. While working I had the issue of accommodation to contend with. I decided to look for a flat once I arrived in Glasgow, as you get a better feel of the place and importantly people you want to move in. The first two weeks were spent at a local hotel, which were fine though not ideal as I am the type of person who needs to be settled to function well. I gave myself two weeks to find somewhere to live and made a number of appointments to view flats in the west end of the city. Surfing the websites, I vividly remember all sites recommending the west end. I still had this perception of Glasgow as a rough place and the murder capital of the UK. How wrong I was to be. Not knowing a soul, I called Ian Wallace, the former Coventry City, Nottingham Forest and Scotland player. Ian lived close to Ibrox and came over almost immediately. He could see I had no idea about Glasgow so he used to take time out in the evenings to show me the different parts of the city. He also came along with me to view the flats. After several weeks of looking, and still with no accommodation, frustration started to set in.

One morning I happened to cross paths with commercial director Imran Ahmad. He asked how I was doing, at which point I just said I was struggling with finding suitable accommodation which as a result was affecting me at work. "Come and stay in my flat; I have a spare room." It transpired the club had a lease on a flat in Hyndland until August. That gave me six months security. Once we agreed my share of the costs, I accepted and moved in within days. The flat was a beautiful tenement, on the third floor without lifts. This was fine for me but Imran would constantly complain, which was understandable as he was not exactly the fittest guy around. I literally had the flat to myself as Imran would only use the flat to sleep in and stayed out most of the days and weekends. The area of Hyndland was idyllic, a beautiful, leafy suburb of Glasgow. What struck me was the greenery and huge tenement buildings reminding me of when Sharon and I visited New York. The local area was full of coffee shops, independent stores, wine bars and fantastic restaurants. The place was alive day and night. This was a sought-after area and I was very fortunate to be residing here. Hyndland can best be described as a Bohemian living quarter occupied by artists, actors, professionals and rich students.

The only issue living in tenements is the car parking. Unless I was back at the flat by 6pm I would be driving around looking for a car park space. This was the only drawback. Not one for regrets but I should have made more of the Hyndland area while living here. The area was extremely quiet, yet only minutes from the bustling Byers Road. Living here, we had the best of both worlds. If I ever move to Glasgow this is the place I would look out for.

For me Glasgow was completely different to what I had first thought. It was a beautiful city with fantastic architecture and the people are genuine. Friendly and talkative, you knew their family history after ten minutes. Once I got lost and stopped for directions. The Glaswegian lad who must have been in his late 20s literally got in the car and said I will take you to where you need to go. When we arrived I offered him money for a taxi but he refused and wished me well. What I didn't realise was he took me to where he needed to go and I was still miles away from my location. Only in Glasgow!

During my first few weeks I drove about trying to find my bearings. In reality Glasgow is not a big city, it's just very densely populated. The city is honoured with three excellent universities, fantastic shopping centres, more bars and restaurants per square mile than I had ever seen. No matter where you travel in Glasgow, you will almost certainly view fantastic buildings that you rarely see in modern cities around the UK. The centre of Glasgow is a hybrid of old and new. The planners have cleverly maintained old listed buildings while merging the new. As a newcomer to Glasgow I was in awe of the place.

Wherever you go in the centre you will find quirky bars and eateries. What struck me is that these places are also busy during the week. Glaswegians certainly know how to enjoy themselves and take life as it comes.

To an outsider this is a city that believes in and cherishes history and traditions. Glasgow is a city where dreams and aspirations are born and nurtured. This is a place that thrives on diversity and challenging the status quo. It is alive and emerging as a possible powerhouse of the UK. New businesses and entrepreneurs emerge every day. The business culture in Glasgow taught me many new lessons and what struck a chord with me was the honesty and openness of the people. Everyone tends to know everyone in some capacity. The last time I felt such a positive edge was in London. Of course Glasgow has its issues and daily grinds like any other city. There are areas where people live in old high-rise flats and are bordering on the poverty line. What stands out for Glasgow in my opinion is the people's resolve and determination. This is how I view the Glaswegians. Opportunities are endless in Glasgow and regeneration is continuous. Hosting the MTV Awards and the success of the Commonwealth games has certainly put the city firmly on the world map and rightly so. Coventry City started me, Watford changed me and Glasgow Rangers was about to make me.

During the first month I devised a timeline of what we needed to do commercially. I was told the department had been stagnant for a while and just needed new ideas to inject some drive and positivity in the sales team.

This was not just about bringing new ideas to the club. It was also about me trying to evolve and push the limits to keep me focussed. The key is to maintain momentum. However, Rangers was like no other club. This was a way of life, as I very quickly found out. If there is a problem at Rangers, there is a problem in the home of every supporter. I can only now describe coming to work at Rangers as attending a public institution. Every word, movement, look, emotion is scrutinised by the local media. They could tell you things about yourself you never knew existed. In the first few weeks I was oblivious to this all. I am sure I was warned, though you tend to think *it's only a football club*, albeit a huge world brand. At first the media attention to the club was overwhelming. Although most football clubs appear on the back pages of a newspaper, Rangers mostly occupied the front. On a regular basis photographers would be waiting outside the reception area to interview the Chairman Charles Green or the manager Ally McCoist. This was all new to me. The only time I would see journalists at my previous clubs were during press conferences and then we could only muster one or two apprentices. Here at Rangers you would think we were about to sign a world class player with the number of journalists congregating outside the ground. Most of the staff at Rangers were used to such media intensity and would ignore the fuss. At first, when the cameras appeared, I would acknowledge the journalists. That was until the Charles Green racism row erupted and I would have photographers looking at me contemplating as to whether I was Imran Ahmad or not. Firstly, I was half the size of him and secondly he was coming in for some bad press and the last thing I needed was to be mistaken for Imran in Glasgow. The safest policy when working for either Rangers or Celtic was actually to stay incognito.

I had several revenue generating ideas. From day one I was buzzing knowing I could implement my vision and ideas that had been a success at my previous clubs. Due to the size of Rangers, in terms of supporters, corporate customers and businesses I was convinced we could generate hundreds of thousands of pounds for the club. I just knew I had the plans that would transform us commercially. Irene was always positive and that gave me the impetus to keep going. I had devised plans for the next three years. Naturally it is important to have people onside from the start. At first everything was positive, though to be fair I had not really tested the water with my new ideas. What I did quickly realise was the embedded, resistant culture in certain departments at the club.

Some of the staff appeared reluctant to entertain or try new ideas. Not being able to push the boundaries naturally curtails any creativity and out of the box thinking. Even those that were outward-looking at the club found themselves locked in a cultural bubble that needed bursting. It was as if we were living in the past. For me we had the opportunity to become commercial pioneers. I am not for one moment saying all my ideas would work. However, they were a starting point. I am a great believer of giving an idea a go if you genuinely believe in the concept. At the very least you can only learn from the experience.

There were some very experienced staff at Rangers. They had the knowledge, acumen and ability to take this club to a higher level. A good leader at the top would have coaxed this out of the staff. For me the greatest asset Rangers had was its employees. They had been at the club for several years and would go through brick walls for Rangers. It was personal, it was their club and they were honoured to work at Ibrox. This is what struck me when I first joined the club. The passion for Rangers was incredible, something I had not seen at many clubs.

As a new employee, I could see the bigger picture. This was not just about personal aspirations; it was also about leaving a commercial legacy for a club that gave me an opportunity such as Coventry and Watford. If businesses think in terms of borders or localities, then that's what you will achieve – local and small. There are no rules or parameters in football or for any other type of business. Our minds create boundaries and limitations. Who's to say a League 2 professional football club cannot have aspirations abroad with countries such as India or China? It's certainly not confined to the top five or six Premiership clubs, though that's what is communicated back to us. The question is who sets the boundaries? At Rangers this may be explained by past decision makers setting the agenda and in time such actions and thoughts become ingrained within the organisation. This in turn dictates the culture of the club. My point here is innovative ideas can become stifled if people are not allowed to challenge or be given the freedom to move forward for the good of the club.

Of course there will be setbacks and I have certainly experienced my fair share. Don't dwell on them, learn to accept what's not worked or been successful and move on. They should merely act as a catalyst to continue to greater things. Martin Edwards, the former CEO of Manchester United, comes to mind. He had the foresight to create a new dawn at United. Aspirations went through the roof and, for many years, on a macro level they led the way on and off the pitch. At Rangers it felt as though we were clinging on to the past. This is not a criticism of the people working there, it's merely an observation. When I did push some people to discuss how they would manage Rangers, suddenly I found them opening up to new ideas. If only people managing the club had the temerity to have an open discussion on how to move forward. Together we had the opportunity of transforming Rangers to become a commercially worldwide proposition with an open-minded organisation. We did not have to try too hard. Supporters and admirers from all over the world would get in touch with me offering their support and advice. The hard work was done. Rangers' supporters would do anything for the club.

The simple solution for the current employees would have been to leave the club for pastures new during liquidation. They decided to stay and help the club. Their loyalty was being tested. After the new takeover I was told they were given little or no information about the club. They had no idea as to whether they would still be required. Put simply, they had given their trust to the new ownership and all they wanted in return was to know what direction the club was going to move towards. Lack of communication, liquidation, media coverage and Rangers being demoted all added to the negativity among some members of staff. In defence of the new management I am not so sure they knew the extent of what they had taken on. I had only joined months after the new management had taken control of Rangers, and even then I sensed they were trying to find their way around the club. They would constantly talk about how the club was always under immense scrutiny. This is when I realised what I had come into and in many ways relished the opportunity.

Each day travelling to and from Ibrox created an exciting feeling of what we could all achieve and where we could take this world brand. We were to begin engaging with all the businesses in the area before widening our scope regionally, nationally and globally. I had communicated new ideas of forming a sister development programme with clubs abroad, allowing us all to leverage maximum partnership funds. Perhaps I was too optimistic or ahead of time of where Rangers currently stood. I wanted to evolve the commercial side and bring some energy to the sponsorships. Times change, people and business leaders change and often ideas implemented differently can and will work. I genuinely felt we could achieve what we wanted at Rangers. With such an enormous and loyal fan base this was a sleeping giant commercially.

We were sitting on a potential gold mine and I was not sure some sections of the senior management team realised this. I understand we were constantly dealing with off-field issues and always responding to media speculation. However, you have to detach yourself from the negative vibes and remain focussed on the bigger picture. This was easier said than done, as you need a leader to steer the ship. There was a fire raging at Ibrox prior to me joining Rangers and you could feel the flames rising each and every day. There was a battle raging which was soon to come to a head.

On the pitch the club, under the management of Ally McCoist, were beating teams at a canter. Home games could not come around quick enough. The buzz on match days was incredible. With over 40,000 season ticket holders in League Three, the attendances were regularly reaching 50,000. The expectations and pressures also came with being at a club like Rangers, especially in the lower leagues. A win was expected, a draw just about tolerable and a defeat would be catastrophic. If anyone could see this period through it had to be Ally McCoist. He galvanised the supporters and built a team that would win games and ultimately the league. I vividly remember the last game of the season against Stranraer. Ally gave a rousing speech in the middle of the pitch after the game to mark Rangers' return to the Championship. It has to be one of the most inspiring motivational talks I have ever heard, in front of over 50,000 supporters. The emotion could be felt around the ground. Ally certainly had this aura and presence about him, but at Rangers he was one of us and always approachable. Admittedly some sections of the supporter base did criticise Ally for not bringing on younger players. On one occasion I remember Ally explaining that playing for Rangers has its own pressures and even some great players who have worn the famous blue shirt have struggled to adapt to the intensity. What he wanted to do was build a team blended with experience and youth that could play without fear and more importantly win games. Ally's remit was to deliver Rangers back into the Premiership as soon as possible. We need to remember he had to win the leagues while ensuring Rangers were promoted at the first time of asking. Looking back to the first and only season in League Three, the team scored 87 goals and only lost three matches. The team hardly had a pre-season and was put together in a space of a few weeks. Anyone who knows Ally will know he gave his all to the cause. We all have our opinions but, for me, he had a thankless task and you could see the pressures he was under during the last few months of his reign. The discontent amongst supporters began during the League One campaign when the style of play was constantly questioned. Such were the expectations Rangers had to win and win in style. For me Ally once again delivered with statistics of winning 33 out of 36 games with no losses and scoring 106 goals! As I have mentioned before, winning games was expected at Rangers – what the supporters wanted was the flair to go with it.

Regarding off the field issues, Imran never discussed the situation at Rangers, though he did give the impression this was an investment and once Rangers were back in the top flight he would look to move on. His family was based in London and we did discuss the practicalities of living in Scotland. We both had young kids so living apart for weeks on end can become difficult. The reasons I moved to Glasgow Rangers was in complete contrast to Imran. For me, this was a positive career move and an opportunity to challenge myself at a club the size of Rangers. It did not surprise me when Imran finally left, albeit in awkward circumstances. One of the incredulous stories that emerged out of the media during this period was about Charles calling Imran his 'little Paki friend'. At first I couldn't get my head around the accusation – after all this was 2013, not the 1980s. I was totally shocked when I read the local papers. Charles almost immediately apologised when realising his mistake. What Charles and Imran do or say in private is their prerogative but in public you are not only discrediting Rangers Football Club, you are offending millions of people. Anyone who has been on the receiving end of racism will understand how bitter and offensive the term Paki still is. The word still conjures up images and memories of the dark days when people would be beaten up because of their colour or religion. Charles just appeared to be completely ignorant to the actual word and offence caused. To appease matters, Imran released a picture of Charles holding Imran's daughter as a way of exonerating Charles from any racist accusations. In all honesty the damage was done.

Everyone at the club sensed that Charles's days were numbered. Within weeks Charles stepped down with only Brian Stockbridge, the club's Finance Director, remaining from the original takeover group. Rumours were rife as to who was going to take over as CEO. There were power struggles within and outside of the club. It just appeared as if everyone wanted a piece of Rangers Football Club. It was stalemate. The hierarchy at the club would not let go and outside forces could not get in. This was a war of attrition with no ending in sight. Within this mental pressure cooker we all had a job to do. What I noticed among the staff in general was everyone pulling together for the good of Rangers Football Club, yet not knowing if they would still be in a job the next day. This was the mental and physical pressure we were all under. However, time and time again it demonstrated the commitment of normal working people who loved Rangers Football Club. This was a way of life; it was their duty to ensure this great institution was not tarnished. Of course there were days when we would all be frustrated from the ongoing issues, this was only natural. Overall I have nothing but admiration for the Glasgow Rangers employees who performed against a backdrop of uncertainty.

Almost immediately after Charles Green's departure, Craig Mather took on the CEO role. Craig was a very likeable guy and much more approachable than Charles. My first encounter with Craig was brief, but he had made an impression immediately. He came across as a very open person who really wanted to make a go of it at Rangers. It was also noted how the staff were more relaxed and looking forward to the future with Craig at the helm. This was down to Craig's leadership. He really did give a good example of how to be a good leader without the need to be seen as a ruthless assassin. All that is just a show for me from people who believe they need to exert their nasty side to gain respect. What they fail to realise is they have lost the respect of their staff before they even begin.

On the pitch, pre-season started very well. There was an air of optimism amongst us all. I remember the first game at home in the Championship where there is the unfurling of the flag. Apparently this is a tradition in Scotland where all the league winning teams are given a Football League flag to unfurl. The atmosphere once again was electric as the opposition was Heart of Midlothian. This was going to be a test against a former Premiership side. Unfortunately Rangers lost and tended to struggle throughout the season against similar opposition. During this period I actually started to enjoy my time at the club. Enjoyment comes in many guises and for me it's being allowed to manage your department and having the autonomy to make decisions. There was even a period of hiatus of the negative media reporting on the club. Not only had we generated much needed revenue with new initiatives, business on the whole was looking up. With such a positive mindset, and believing we could achieve anything at Rangers, we were beginning to attract substantial investment from various organisations. The interest suddenly increased. At Rangers we were all full of optimism for the forthcoming season.

It also helps when the people you are working for give you their full backing to be creative and Irene for me was an excellent manager. She never took sides and was straight down the line. You knew where you stood with Irene. For me Irene would have been the perfect CEO for Rangers Football Club. This was a person who showed compassion when needed, could be tough as nails when the situation required and had a very measured approach to business. The plans for the future were in place, we just needed the go ahead from above. Unfortunately off the pitch issues put paid to most of our ideas. It is extremely difficult to exert any influence with the Directors when there is a constant merry-go-round of owners and Chief Executives. We were literally starting all over again almost every six months such was the instability at the top.

While on the pitch we had a very successful start to the season, off the pitch issues continued to dominate the headlines. Craig Mather resigned as CEO in October 2013 after a short tenure. With Charles and Imran resigning a few months earlier we were left with one board member in Brian Stockbridge. Brian was targeted by Rangers supporters for a lack of transparency over club contracts and off the field deals. Brian came into Rangers with Charles and Imran and many of the club supporters were suspicious of the consortium they were representing. It was never revealed and this added to the rumours and a lack of trust. For a period of three to four months it felt we were completely rudderless. Graham Wallace was eventually installed as the new CEO.

The AGM was organised prior to Christmas. This became the focal point for all the staff. We were all given duties and security on the day was tight. I remember the Head of Security, big John Allan, introducing me to two plain clothes officers who were from special branch. This is how serious the issue at Rangers had become. They knew the perpetrators and wanted to ensure the event had no incidents. The day itself was exciting. Thousands of shareholders attended, young and old. The stage was designed to face the Main Stand seating area. As each of the Directors made their way to the stage the booing became louder and louder. To be a Director on the day was not for the faint hearted. Graham Wallace and Ally McCoist were the only two to walk away without any heckling or booing. As an outsider you could sense the frustration and anger amongst the supporters. These are people who have supported their club all of their lives and felt it was being mismanaged by Directors who had very little or no knowledge of Rangers and were not Rangers men. The supporters demanded transparency over one particular area of who owned shares in Margarita Holdings and Blue Pitch Holdings. Charles Green was despised by many and a number of supporters felt he still had an influence by way of the shareholding. This set the scene for 2014 as we embarked on another year of mistrust, frustration, anger and a division between the supporters and the club.

The Christmas period of 2013 was spent at home in Coventry. I always found coming home gave me a sense of peace with the pressure lifted from my shoulders. Coming home re-energised and vitalised me. At times I could feel the pressure dissipating as soon as I left Glasgow. This was the enormity of the club and the role in difficult circumstances. However, each time I came home to visit the family I had this overwhelming urge to get back to Glasgow and keep going. It gets hold of you like a tight grip that you cannot loosen. You want to improve everything within your remit. One of my colleagues, Jack, lived in Stratford-upon-Avon, a half hour drive from my house. We agreed to travel back together after celebrating the Christmas period with our respective families. That has to be the quietest journey back to Glasgow. Both of us hardly spoke for five and a half hours as the thought of going back into the pressure cooker must have been at the forefront for the both of us. This is the impact a club in trouble the size of Rangers can have on any individual. My experience and always setting myself goals has helped me remain focused on many occasions but this was something new to me. However, no matter how difficult the situation at Rangers, I was determined to give it my best.

Jack and I shared a flat in Glasgow Harbour. A large two bedroom flat that was on the doorstep of Dumbarton Road and a 10 minute walk from Byres Road, which had some great bars and restaurants. The occasions I was staying over during the weekend we would make a visit to the Gumbo Bar on Byres Road. Saturday was a live band night where music varied from rock n roll to rhythm and blues. These were great times and memories where you could enjoy the music and for a short while forget the issues at Rangers.

Glasgow really was thriving and appeared to have the foresight to build for the future without losing its identity. In many respects Glasgow epitomised a European city with all the history, architecture, museums and of course the ample number of bars and restaurants. Towards the end of my tenure I did make a concerted effort to visit the museums and attractions. This is the only city I know where the police are visible and ready to let you know who's in charge. As an old Glaswegian once said to me, the police are the new gangsters in town.

I remember one night walking back from the Gumbo Bar situated on Byers Road late at night and police were standing almost all the way down Dumbarton Street. As expected for a late night, people were loud and revellers were singing but one thing that struck me was nobody was causing any trouble. There was no intimidation or watching your back. This was Glasgow and I felt very safe, unlike some cities I can think of. While Jack and I did not take the time to visit some of the well-known bars in the West End, we did make a habit of meeting at the St Louis Café on the corner of Dumbarton Road. The café/bar was opposite the Glasgow Harbour and yet it took us months before we eventually decided to make a visit. It was a very student-looking place but a great venue to unwind and relax. We spent a few good nights in the bar enjoying the music, which was as diversified as the regulars. It was here where I had also been introduced to Gordon, my opposite at Celtic, through a mutual friend. We became good friends and would share business and commercial ideas. There was a good rapport between staff at Rangers and Celtic and had been for several years. If a company tried to play one off the other we would inform our counterparts. Commercially and at our level we had a great respect for one another.

Not being the greatest of chefs, I would regularly frequent Mr Singh's, an Indian Restaurant in Charing Cross close to Glasgow city centre. Either on a Friday night or after a home game at Ibrox I would make my way to Mr Singh's. The well known Satty Singh, the owner and huge Rangers fan, became a good friend. I also got on very well with his two sons who were named after Rangers players. One was named after Mark Walters and the other Oleg Kuznetsov. Apparently during one particular Rangers match Satty vowed to name his new born son after the next Rangers player to score a goal.

Unfortunately for his son, Oleg Kuznetsov scored and Satty remained true to his word. It took weeks to convince me as I believed Mark was short for Manjit or something similar and Oleg, well he must be the only Indian on earth with such a name on his birth certificate! Satty was always around if ever I needed company or time out. For someone who knows his curries, Mr Singh's is one of the best Indian Restaurants I have dined at. The food is authentic and can easily pass for home cooking. Throw in the typical Glaswegian hospitality and you have the best of everything.

It is interesting how music can define a period in one's life. During my stay in Glasgow the music that kept me motivated or was relevant to my time there was the Stone Roses. While I am open to various genres of music, the Stone Roses just fitted in with my life in Glasgow. There are many occasions when the Roses' music was almost therapeutic and removed me from the real issues I had to deal with at Rangers.

2014 started off well; we were winning games on the pitch and business was healthy off it. Even with the new management I remained positive that they could provide me and my colleagues with the autonomy and tools to keep up the progressive work we had started. Graham Wallace was appointed with an experienced background and offered hope to us all. He needed time to implement and develop his plans. He pointed out at the AGM in December that he wanted 120 days to carry out a thorough assessment of the club. What he probably did not realise was that he would be held to every word. Supporters had even created a stopwatch to monitor his 120 days. As each day passed he was constantly reminded of the time he had remaining. This became like an obsession; suddenly this 120 day review was all that was being discussed. The Scottish media were having a field day. I actually felt for Graham as I am sure he wanted to genuinely buy time to offer a comprehensive review of the club. Of course he knew the issues, though he probably wanted to also offer manageable solutions. The supporters had been humiliated, lied to and now wanted answers. They had every right to feel the way they were. In the local media and on radio we were reminded almost daily that we were working for a new Ranger. It soon catches up with you and in a place like Glasgow, where reputations mean everything, the board had to deliver irrespective of the current incumbents. Graham had his work cut out and he had only been there two minutes. Such was the intensity on the outcome of the review I am sure Graham gave this more time than required to appease the supporters.

Prior to the report being published, Graham appointed a number of his close confidantes on an interim basis. For me this was a positive move, as the culture of the club needed re-energising and I believed new blood would help bring about change. To be fair to most of the staff, there was a general consensus that the new appointments can only be good for the club. There will always be negative comments, which I believe are borne out of fear and insecurity. While the business continued as normal on a day to day basis we were absolutely sure plans were being made behind the scenes. The 120 day report was almost at halfway point. Irene remained my manager, though we both knew change was coming. However, Irene, as I have said, will always have my respect for being a professional throughout the changes. On the pitch Ally McCoist could do no more as Rangers literally ran away with the league. Just a couple of draws upset the league table though I am sure Ally was satisfied with a job well done. The atmosphere at the club was much more positive. Supporters had backed Graham and were waiting in earnest for his report. Commercially, we were doing extremely well, performing above targets.

There was definitely an air of optimism.

The day of reckoning had almost arrived. Just prior to issuing the 120 day report Graham called a meeting to address the staff about his vision and to discuss elements of the report. The meeting was on Friday yet on the Thursday, a day before the meeting, one of the Rangers shareholders made a comment to the local media that Rangers would struggle with funds if supporters failed to back the club. You can imagine the rumour mill going into overdrive. The media once again was waiting outside the Ibrox reception as staff arrived to work in the morning. The media camping outside Ibrox became part of normal life. All the staff made their way to the Ibrox Lounge on Friday lunchtime to be addressed by Graham. We all had our own versions and opinions of what was going to be said. As humans we are so creative when hit with adversity. Most don't realise they could become crime novelists with their imagination running wild.

Graham began discussing the report, highlighting the fundamental areas of the cost base and the need to restructure the club. He also announced the club would be going through a redundancy process as part of the restructuring. At this point you could hear a pin drop. Another round of redundancies for staff would be the tipping point for many. Sometimes tough decisions have to be made and to be honest I remained upbeat as the commercial department, in my opinion, is a revenue generator and the last place to be on someone's redundancy radar. I had been through this procedure before. Now was not the time to lose faith.

Understandably this shook many of the employees. To make matters worse our programme supplier refused to deliver programmes for the Saturday home fixture thinking we had gone into administration. This all came about because of comments by a shareholder on Thursday followed by a staff meeting on the Friday.

The media knew about the staff meeting before we did. Many of our customers thought the staff meeting was to inform us of the club going into administration once again. I did think of calling the press to get a sneak preview of what Graham would be discussing! In all honesty Graham chose certain aspects of the report that he felt were appropriate. The report was slammed for being too short and non-detailed. The lesson learned was never put a timescale on a report. The longer the time span, the higher the expectations. The media and the supporters were vitriolic in their condemnation of the report for lacking real detail and not really answering any fundamental questions. One critic commented that their office junior could have completed the report in an afternoon. An over-exaggeration, though point taken. In my opinion Graham Wallace was an excellent appointment and given time and resources would definitely have brought Rangers back to its glory days.

However, at Rangers you are never too far away from upheaval. I broke up for annual leave on Tuesday 21st October 2014 and was travelling to France with the family for a short break. I left the club with Graham Wallace as CEO, Philip Nash as Financial Director and Richard Berry as Chief Commercial Officer. On my return to London on Saturday 25th October I was informed by my brother-in-law Billy Gill that there had been a major change at Rangers. I was quite blasé about the whole situation. After all, this was Rangers and I expect some change on a regular basis. It's only when Billy explained that Philip had resigned and Graham was on his way out that I nearly fell off my chair. In the space of three days the club had literally changed hands. It had transpired that Mike Ashley had an option of having a nominated Director on the board. This was taken up by Derek Llambias, who had worked with Mike at Newcastle United. When it finally dawned that

I was returning to a new regime my mind went into overdrive. It's amazing how constant change leaves you with a series of emotions from feeling empty, shocked, nervous and then to feeling excited and optimistic all in a short space of time. One minute you are on a high the next on a low as the emotions spin from one extreme to another. As humans I feel we are conditioned to fear the worst and this can be a difficult emotion to remove. As I have mentioned previously whenever I am faced with a negative situation I try and develop a positive attitude. This is a trait that has been with me from a young age. That's not to say every issue turns out to be fine, I just have a coping mechanism that kicks in. I do believe we are all in control of our destiny to some extent and can make the change to improve our lives if we want to. The choice is with us. Our minds are wonderful creatures that need constant training and affirmations. The old adage of seeing the glass half full comes to mind. Working at Rangers was almost like being at an educational establishment by using all kinds of techniques to overcome fear, keeping a positive attitude and not giving into external negative thoughts. I probably honed my life skills more during my time at Rangers than with my previous two employers and this during my first few weeks of being there!

Living in Glasgow minus the family gave me plenty of time to think and because I had no distractions I began meditating, enabling me to have the peace of mind to remove myself from the pressure cooker of working at Rangers. I also decided to pursue an idea to develop a programme for players as their careers were coming to an end. I mooted the idea with Gordon Taylor, the CEO of the PFA, who gave me the opportunity to present my case to his colleagues. I made my way to the PFA offices in Manchester to put my proposal forward. I genuinely felt I had a chance of success as I was experienced in the industry and this would also be seen as a positive move from the PFA. I met with Gordon and his colleagues and began to explain the proposal I developed, which was to improve the employment prospects of former players. The idea was to coach the players with basic fundamental sales skills with the idea of then placing these players with the clubs they currently play or have played with. Working in the commercial or other departments not only keeps the player at the club but ensures they do not have to uproot their family and can maintain a sense of stability. The benefit for the club is a former player equipped to generate revenue and from a PR perspective is a win-win situation. I was generally optimistic of the outcome after all this was an organisation that is founded on the welfare of current and former players. The ethos of the PFA is to support and engage with former players.

Unfortunately their resources were at a premium even though the initial response was extremely positive. I have to give Gordon praise for meeting me and making the necessary introductions. I will always respect him for always making the effort to respond to me. After all, he must be inundated with people trying to make contact with him. I still believe in the concept and will one day revisit my plans of how to launch the programme with the support of the PFA or related governing bodies.

THE FINAL COUNTDOWN

Another change at Rangers, what's next I thought driving back to Glasgow? I started to think of my next plan. My mind was racing 100 miles an hour thinking of what my next challenge could be. The point with me is I need to sometimes slow down and take stock of what I really want to do. I know at times I frustrate the people close to me as I am like a whirlwind who wants to take on the world. That's just me letting off my enthusiasm and vision. Of course I am aware you have to take life one step at a time, but why hold someone back when the one idea could be the game changer.

The next day I was full of anticipation as to how the landscape was changing. Again there was an air of expectation, though generally it never does turn out as you expect. As usual the staff began making their predictions of what was going to happen next. Me, I was not sure this time how I felt. Again my intuition was telling me this time around we were in for a tough time. At this stage I had not even met David Somers or Derek Llambias. I just harboured this feeling that we were all in for a bumpy ride. It may seem obvious with what had been going on at Rangers over the last two to three years. However, when a new ownership arrives with pockets as deep as Mike Ashley's, you would expect everyone connected with Rangers to be jubilant. Not at Rangers; I can honestly say all the staff felt nervous. It's as if we all just knew the consequences. We could write the script. The waiting game was over when we received an email from Chairman David Somers's PA that he wanted to meet all the managers that morning. The meeting took place in the boardroom. It was a quiet sombre atmosphere. It's like being summoned by the President of your country to explain how we have lost another key battle somewhere in the world. In reality we had lost the battle and the war. There was complete silence when David walked in. David can best be described as an English aristocrat who would not look out of place at Eton. His opening gambit to explain another change at Rangers was to describe how his wife had just bought a Grade 2 listed building over the weekend without his knowledge. The point he was making was sometimes, you are faced with situations you have no control over and have to deal with them accordingly. Looking around the room we understood his point, but to let us in on the fact his wife had just bought a Grade 2 listed building was probably a bad example. These were hardcore Glaswegians he was talking to, not City brokers from London.

He explained how there were three parties at the table, Mike Ashley, Brian Kennedy and Dave King. All three were asked to provide proof of funds. It must be noted that several of my colleagues and supporters I had spoken to wanted Dave King as the new owner. As explained to me, he was a Rangers man and one of the few people they could trust to restore the club's reputation.

David Somers in closing addressed us all by stating Derek Llambias and Barry Leach were merely consultants and we were not to be intimidated by them. Those words alone set the alarm bells ringing.

Unfortunately we never met David Somers again as the axe began falling on the administrative staff. Two days after David addressed the managers Derek Llambias began to assert his presence and within a week David Somers had literally disappeared.

This time round you could see and feel the fear and frustration affecting most of the employees. *This time will be different* was the common saying among the Rangers employees. For some reason I had an awkward feeling the new regime would be ruthless. One of the staff members who had just been made redundant was pre-warning us all to be on our guard. These are not normal people who will care about the club or the staff. They care about the pounds and nothing else. This was Rangers Football Club, not a financial institution. The fans know exactly what is happening at the club. Some even knew about confidential dealings before we the senior management found out. I remember phoning an ardent Rangers supporter to get the low down on what was going on at the club. He was also the one who informed me there would be mass redundancies at Rangers weeks before they were announced.

It was on Wednesday 5th November, Bonfire Day of all days, when we had our meeting with David Somers. By Friday 7th November Derek Llambias was calling the shots. On the Saturday we were playing Alloa at Ibrox and this is the first time I was introduced to Derek. He was courteous and appeared to be a down-to-earth character. Unbeknown to me there was to be one further meeting which I was not prepared for.

On Monday 10th November all seemed quiet at the club. My attitude was to remain calm and just keep performing to the best of my ability. Everything else was out of my control. Whatever was going on in the background I tried to not let it distract me. The rumour mill started again on Wednesday 12th November about a major meeting with Derek and some of the Directors who we directly reported to. This was a meeting that continued until early evening so most of us would not find out the details until the next morning. On Thursday 13th November, I received an early morning email from Irene stating she wanted to see all the commercial team to give us an update of the meeting the previous evening. At the time only the commercial administrator and I were present. Irene stated that there were to be staff cuts though assured us we would be fine as the two of us had valuable knowledge that the club could ill afford to lose. Due to one of my colleagues being on maternity leave we desperately needed cover. Over the previous couple of weeks we had interviewed several potential Sales Executives. The day before we were about to make a formal offer to one of the interviewees an email from David Somers clearly stated we could not hire any new recruits until further notice. The warning signs were looming.

In the morning Irene is telling us our jobs were secure and by late afternoon a colleague is interrupting my meeting requesting to see me urgently. David Somers's PA had called to say I was needed in the Chairman's office sooner rather than later. I duly finished the meeting, which was coming to an end, and made my way to see David Somers, or so I thought. My colleague looked at me horrified as if something was wrong. I was much more laid back and thought they must need further information on the commercial aspects of the club. Entering the Chairman's room, I saw Derek sat at one side of the table and on the opposite side to him the HR consultant. Immediately I sensed bad news. Derek literally said they had conducted a review and unfortunately I was no longer to be part of the club moving forward. I would be put on garden leave for two weeks and paid my notice period and any holiday owing. I was not sure about other members of staff, but for me the consultation, that I never knew about, lasted less than two minutes. Derek had never spoken to me prior to this meeting other than to request some information and had no understanding of what I had achieved in my two years at Rangers or had in the pipeline. In less than two years I had sourced the club's new shirt sponsor and negotiated several partnerships during one of the most challenging and difficult times in Rangers' history. Yet he never once made an effort to question me or ask for my opinion. Their minds were clearly made up. It's never pleasant to be told you are losing your job so close to Christmas, but do it with some respect and dignity. No pre-warning, nor any support. You couldn't make it up but then this is the football industry. I know if the previous full time HR Manager was still at Rangers the situation would have been handled more professionally. I did mention a minor detail that I was owed commission for sourcing the shirt sponsorship. Derek literally shrugged at the idea of having to pay me anything more besides my notice period. Redundancies unfortunately are a part of working life. Most people will experience it at some time during their career. While there were only a handful of redundancies, for some reason the hatchet appeared to fall on the commercial department with myself and two other colleagues the victims. Most of the other departments survived any cuts. We were the commercial hub of the club and generating revenue so I could not understand and was never told why our department was severely hit. We never did find out as within a month Derek himself departed from the club. To think if we had survived another month we may still have been at Rangers. What also made the episode difficult was that I had personally been speaking to major organisations from India with the support of one of the government ministers in the UK. I was fluent in the Indian language and with a settled club we had the opportunity to maximise the Rangers brand abroad, and especially in South-East Asia. These are the moments when you think of what if?

Naturally I was despondent, but a decision had been made and there was nothing I could do to reverse the outcome. In a situation like this I just tried to remain calm and measured. As I had experienced this previously, I made sure I took all my belongings and did not leave anything behind when leaving Ibrox Stadium. I also made a point of saying my goodbyes to my colleagues knowing full well I would not be allowed back in the building while Derek was at the helm. While it was a strange feeling to leave in essence for the last time, I also felt the pressure lifted from my shoulders. I immediately drove to Murray Park, Rangers' training ground, to say my farewell to the staff based there. Ally McCoist was actually in a team meeting when I arrived. Not having much time I knocked on his door to thank him for his support. He knew something was not right and immediately postponed the meeting. We chatted for quite a while about the strife at Rangers. You could see in his eyes he was genuinely sad for all the staff. Before I left he asked me to stay in touch and if he could help with references or anything else to simply call him. Ally will always have my utmost respect as he understands the common man. He justifies the word legend. What struck me with the Rangers' staff on and off the pitch and what sets this club apart from most, if not all, is there are no prima donnas. They are simply not tolerated at Rangers. I have been at clubs where average players behave as if they are world class internationals. At Rangers, every employee is on the same level and this was demonstrated each time I visited the training ground. Ally McCoist and his staff and the current set of players treated you with respect, hence the reason they commanded respect from us all.

I just needed to get away from my flat as I had too much thinking time. I spent the evening discussing the day's events with my close pal Kash Taank, who always made time for me during my stay in Glasgow. In the morning I could not wait to leave – everything was a rush. The drive home was not one of my best, especially as I had five hours of thinking time! The music was on, though I could not say which album was being played. Luckily I had taken the Best of The Smiths out of the CD player the previous week. I was continuously thinking about what had just occurred and how this would now impact my life. No more, I kept saying to myself. Now is the time to take the leap of faith and finally go it alone. Of course I had some amazing friends and associates who would do anything for me. Now was the time to call on their expertise; deep down my instincts kept telling me to form my own company. Never again will I put myself in a position to be exploited. Neither will I be at the behest of someone else making life changing decisions on my behalf. It's just the way I felt at the time. This is not the way I will ever do business or treat people. Within a week of arriving home, I rejoined the Lions Gym. The raw energy and ideas came flooding back as I was about to embark on another journey in my life.

BEHIND THE SCENES
IN FOOTBALL –
THE REALITY

Having now worked in the football industry for over 22 years, I have the utmost respect for anyone employed in the industry for a length of time. Irrespective of their role or status I know, having led a working life dedicated to the industry, how difficult and challenging any position can be. For a start very few clubs invest in their own staff. Many learn as they go along, a kind of on the job training. You can forget about a trade union – in the football industry you really are on your own. Organised chaos best sums up many of the clubs I have worked at. From the moment I walked in to the Chairman's office at Coventry requesting an opportunity, to twenty years later dealing with the pressure cooker at Glasgow Rangers, you are constantly tested. It's the nature of the beast. Just as there is a merry-go-round with managers the situation is almost the same off the pitch. Until recently most senior employees would expect to remain with a club for several years. Now I am witnessing change at the top more frequently, as the challenges behind the scenes become much more demanding. There are daily struggles, political manoeuvring and pressures to achieve targets which then become reassessed mid-season in line with increased spending. Either way, someone has to deal with the shortfall and that normally makes its way down to the commercial departments. Over the years I have seen so many people employed by football clubs in various positions leave within weeks and, in some cases, days. They arrive with a completely skewed perception of how the industry operates. On the pitch is where most if not all the resources are concentrated. The challenge off the pitch can be very demanding and intense and is certainly not for the faint hearted. It's like a throwback to the working days of the 70s and 80s. You are constantly under pressure to perform. Football is fluid and you need to be entrepreneurial and creative. You are almost reinventing yourself and the direction of the club every two to three years, such are the demands to keep pace with Premiership clubs and technology. It's almost an impossible task as you are dealing with severely limited resources and a club that is way off the radar for the global corporations. I always explain to new recruits entering the world of football for the very first time not to expect the glamorous life. That is a figment of people's imagination. Such a world does not exist unless you are the owners of the clubs. For six days a week you will be expected to work your ass off to bring in as much revenue as possible and then more. The real enjoyment is looking forward to the home matches. All the work and effort comes to fruition on a match day. That's the easy part of working at a football club.

As mentioned earlier, the crux of the season is prepared in a period of three to four months during the summer. The remainder of the season is to fill the gaps by way of hospitality and match day sponsorships or partnerships. Then there is the issue of increasing season ticket sales and generating as much revenue for new kit sales. It really is full on. You will not be sat with the Club Manager on a Monday morning having coffee discussing tactics for the next home fixture. The reality is you will be working to unrealistic targets to sell out a Tuesday night game against an unpopular side nobody wants to watch. That is life in the Championship and below. You have to live, breathe and shit football 24/7. There are no short measures. If you really want to be a success then you must be prepared to make the sacrifices. Unfortunately this can equate to not being able to lead a proper family life and only seeing the kids late evenings. By Sunday you are absolutely shattered with your mind in overdrive for the forthcoming week. It's a relentless position that many in the outside world have no idea about.

I always consider myself and some of the others I have met in the industry as mavericks. The staff will always be on edge, conjuring up new initiatives, excitedly looking forward to the difficult Tuesday evening matches. Football can take over your life; it can become an obsession. It gets hold of you and grips you so tight you cannot even contemplate changing jobs or moving to a completely new industry with actual career prospects. The maverick in me views life as a challenge, to always be moving forward and reigniting the burning ambition to succeed. Just as football is a fluid industry we as commercial people all follow suit. Each day is completely different to the next. In many respects we are not even in control of our product, yet we take customers on an emotional rollercoaster each season. They buy into our desperation and persuasiveness. The fervour grips us all and is so powerful I have sold executive boxes, major partnerships and season tickets simply on emotion. What else do we have when your club is going through a crisis? Most football clubs, unlike most industries, trade insolvent and yet no one bats an eyelid. There are not many industries I can think of where the wages of employees is more than 100% of gross turnover. Yet each season the shareholders rejoice when the debt has not increased significantly even though they will never see a dividend. In another industry in similar circumstances these same characters would be up in arms campaigning for the CEO to resign! This is football, the sport we cherish, enjoy and is our national heritage.

Your club, the hub of the community, is always in the public eye. This by nature creates no end of problems for customer facing staff. I have been lectured by supporters for the purchase of players they did not want. They want my opinion and reasons why. I represent the club and so in their eyes should know all the ins and outs. The truth is most of us will not have a clue what the board is discussing and most of the time they don't give a shit what we think either. It is very rare for the board to gauge the opinions of their staff. This is life for the employees in football: exciting, adventurous, on edge and never knowing what the next day brings. Normal people will end up in care homes. Us football people will probably end up in mental homes! I cannot think of many other industries where the product changes almost on a daily basis. In the lower reaches of the leagues there is certainly less consistency in all manners of the business. It's almost living and breathing on a day to day basis. The intensity, mental and physical pressures to succeed are immense. That's why in my opinion I feel most people working in the football industry would struggle to cope with the so-called normal life outside of the game. Likewise, I cannot think of many employees successful in their own respective industry would last two hours at a football club, never mind a day. How would they cope without rules and regulations? There's no such thing as consultations or text book rules to follow for redundancies in football. Put simply it's a two minute meeting and off you go. Very rarely does anybody even question the decision. That's life, move on. That's the maverick in us all. Even lieu days are contested in some clubs where the CEOs expect you to work through match days and see this as some sort of reward for running off your feet all afternoon. While working at Watford I remember leaving home at 6.00am in the morning and not arriving back home until after 8.00pm in the evenings. For weekday evening fixtures I would not arrive back home until the early hours of the morning and then be back up for 6.00am. This was my life for over four years, six days a week. Yet Watford gave me one of my most enjoyable experiences in life. The adrenaline kept me going, though looking back I am not sure how I did keep going for so long. Yet deep in my inner soul I love the excitement of attempting to plan my destination from one day to the next. You have absolutely no control over your business yet you have to perform regardless.

TIME FOR CHANGE

Due to my background in sport I am constantly questioned about the dearth of Asians in British football on and off the pitch. Is the lack of representation due to discrimination, or other untoward reasons? There are certain factors that need to be highlighted, challenged and addressed. However, I will try and offer a balanced view from my personal experiences of how the industry operates – which is not always what it appears to be when on the outside looking in.

On the pitch we are already witnessing a significant number of more Asian players at Academy and youth level than ever before. This has as much to do with British-born Asian parents who understand and respect the professional game to encourage their kids to play as is the development and increase of BAME (Black, Asian & Minority Ethnic) coaches and monitoring of the sport at inception.

It is well documented that several years ago many football coaches harboured stereotypical views about the Asian diet, mentality and ability to progress in the sport. Those are clearly outdated assumptions. The new generation of Asian parents are much more attuned to a career in professional football. They understand the rewards are much higher than some of the traditional academic professions. However, the risks are still apparent, and that applies to all kids dreaming of becoming professional footballers. It's still a fact that over 95% of aspiring Academy players will not make the grade as a professional footballer. Though a breakthrough in my eyes is the day we read a player's name on the team sheet in the Premiership as opposed to making up the numbers in the reserves or youth teams.

Behind the scenes the situation is different. Once you're established in the system you realise the dynamics change, which is why certain factors that influence decision-making need to be challenged and addressed if we are to open the industry to the BAME community and the wider community outside football. Recruitment of people you know of or are familiar with is common. While I have been fortunate to have carved out a successful career in the industry I have been a beneficiary and a victim of such a practice.

One particular incident I remember was meeting a director of a football governing body who told me to apply for one of two senior positions that was about to be advertised. A recruitment firm was hired to oversee the selection process. Each time I called and spoke to the director I was told my CV had been forwarded to the recruitment agency and to expect a call soon. The call never came. I became even more determined. Several attempts later I finally received a call from the recruitment consultant, literally giving me days to submit a piece of work which other candidates had been allowed a month to prepare for. I ensured the work was completed in time so as not to allow the recruitment firm or the governing body an excuse to dismiss me at the first hurdle. A week later the agency phoned to say I would not be progressing to the interview stages due to not completing any seven figure deals at the clubs I had worked for. Surely this was about the ability to perform the role. I would not let this lie and finally the recruitment consultant confessed that the director had already chosen the candidate before the interview process had even begun. As far as the governing body was concerned they had followed the correct procedures.

On another occasion I recall sending my CV online to several high-profile sports agencies and, with my experience and knowledge in the game, expected at least one call. I even kept contact with many of the recruitment consultants on a regular basis. There was always something on the horizon that never quite materialised. While I cannot prove any wrongdoing, I was baffled when I called a particular CEO at a well-known football club who was equally bemused I did not apply for a senior role that was advertised with a particular agency. The agency acting on their behalf selected the candidates they believed were appropriate but failed to include my CV!

The aspect of transparency, accountability and accessibility irrespective of your colour, religion, gender or disability is essential for progress in the sport. With this in mind, I would advocate a regulation whereby all football clubs and governing bodies have to advertise all roles from middle management upwards on a dedicated website. With the F.A. constantly sending out messages about the need for more diversity in the game another platform could be developed to run alongside the new regulation.

One of my proposals would be to create a framework where candidates from the BAME community can forward their CV without being concerned about their name, ethnicity or gender and have the confidence of knowing they will be treated equally. A pipeline of experienced candidates would eventually be created. Think of it as a type of not-for-profit recruitment firm, though with a panel made up with representatives from the F.A., Premier League, English Football League and those from the BAME community who actually work in the industry. In essence this would help clubs to become more reflective of the communities they serve and remove the proverbial ceiling. Any football club or governing body looking to recruit a senior executive can still work with recruitment agencies, though they would also have to inform the panel who can filter and put forward suitable candidates. Clubs will not be under any pressure to interview the selected candidates or offer them employment. However, it will provide transparency and enable the panel to monitor and report on facts rather than assumptions. A yearly audit would reveal the number of senior positions that became available, the number of candidates selected for interview, the number actually interviewed and offered positions. Those not offered an interview or a position would be given feedback. Essentially this would be the first steps to some form of transparency.

On the flip side, as much as this is a challenge to clubs, we are also challenging potential applicants to step forward and make themselves available. There are several professionals from the BAME community occupying senior roles outside of the football or sporting industry. Therefore, in theory, qualified candidates are available should they wish to pursue a career in the sport. The two initiatives running side by side may just encourage clubs and governing bodies to be more transparent and offer equal employment opportunities to all irrespective of colour, race, gender or religion. This would also hopefully root out any stereotypes or unconscious bias certain decision makers may harbour. In my opinion, and as witnessed, a diverse organisation offers a different way of thinking, encourages creativity and potentially reaches out to a wider audience. Importantly all appointments must be based on merit.

During the 80s, when I began attending away matches, some of the places we visited were intimidating for Asian and Black supporters. Racism and hooliganism was rife, which put many of these supporters off attending games. It's only recently that we are beginning to see many more Asian and Black supporters at football matches. I believe several factors, such as the inception of the Premiership, Sky investment, campaign groups, foreign ownership, football in the community, governing bodies and the sport becoming globalised commercially has contributed to clubs openly condemning and making an example of antisocial behaviour. We have also witnessed players who are prepared to stand up for their colleagues, and all these factors combined eventually sends a message to supporters that certain types of behaviour will not be tolerated on or off the pitch.

In my opinion, and as I have personally witnessed, sport is one of the few institutions that can break down barriers and stereotypes. These are the same conversations I have had with Naz Ali at Accrington Stanley, Harj Hir at Leicester City and Zaf Iqbal at Crystal Palace. With over 60 years of experience between us we have probably achieved more for race relations and challenging misconceptions than most organisations I can think of. We socialise and deal with people at all levels all the time. Collectively we have managed to find common ground amongst many of the players, staff, supporters and clients.

It is also important to understand that while football is a global business, and reported on a 24/7 basis, as an industry it is quite small and this increases the competition for available positions. Unlike other industries where there are generally several positions to apply for, football by nature is limited in what it can offer. There are only a select number of high-profile positions available. The question that needs to be addressed is whether there is transparency and access for all. While debate on race is healthy, it can also be counter-productive if it's not measured and balanced. Irrespective of our opinions we must not lose sight of the fact that sport has the ability to galvanise communities.

DARE TO DREAM

During the month of December I was busy organising my flat in Glasgow and paying any outstanding bills. It was also a good time to refocus. Do I look for another football club or create my own sports consultancy? I had begun planning my future for several months prior to leaving Rangers. Kieran Cannon, one of my colleagues at Rangers, and I would spend hours in the evening developing a road map of how and what our plan would look like. The company would be a global success. My journey would take in America, Europe and Asia. The idea was to engage world-wide brands with sporting clubs for mutual benefit. Having worked in the sports industry for many years, I knew exactly what brands were missing out on and what clubs were failing to offer. This would be a win-win situation for both partners. The opportunities were endless. Spiritually I feel everything happens for a reason. The more and more I thought about my future the more I became convinced it was the right time to take the plunge and go it alone. I had the experience, knowledge, credibility and determination to make this a success. There were many associates who I knew would support me in my early days to get the business off the ground. Deep down in my heart I knew if I didn't take the chance now I will regret this for the rest of my life.

For months at Glasgow Rangers I would visualise what I could achieve if I was working for myself. Naturally there is the question of financial security due to family commitments. However, going beyond the monetary issue, I am creating a new world where I am in control of my destiny. The fear of not taking a risk as opposed to becoming fearful of the unknown continually played on my mind. The world is ours to live, learn and take on new challenges.

From a very young age I have always been a dreamer. There is nothing wrong in dreaming. It gives you a mental picture of what you can become. It negates the limiting beliefs to what you can aspire to. My mind was completely made up I was going to go ahead and form Arena Red. This was a huge step for me, a leap of faith as I had no income coming into the household. The bills and mortgage still had to be paid. Yet I continued to have this incredible underlying urge to continue with my plans. My emotions were a mix of excitement, positivity and being totally energised. I am sure there is a euphoric moment in anyone's lives when you finally make a life-changing decision. Such an emotion is normally short-lived before reality hits home and you go back to the comfort zone. There will be and have been pitfalls, though I see them as obstacles that can be removed and put down to experience. I see myself on a journey towards a destination; though I am never sure if I will ever reach it as the journey never really comes to an end. You reach your destination and then you build a new one to keep going and to continue life's challenge of reaching new heights. From the moment I started school to the present day my life has been about giving, challenging myself and not to give up in the face of adversity. Always one to congratulate others on their success and to genuinely celebrate in their achievements, I am also lucky to have similar friends who have been there to support me. Life can be complicated or simple – you have the choice to live the life you want. This is the life I have now chosen and the journey I am about to embark upon. For a number of years I have hungered for the freedom and autonomy to allow my creative side to flourish. I want to be in complete control of my destiny and in doing so spread my wings to achieve my personal and professional ambitions. Going alone involves courage and the temerity to remain positive when times are difficult. While I have absolute faith my project will be successful, there is also a side to me that knows the risks involved. It gives you an adrenaline rush knowing your fate is in your own hands.

January 1st 2015 was to be the day I began my new journey into the unknown. With no income the pressure was on. I just felt that what I was doing was right. After all, I have generated millions for football clubs. I somehow knew I would find a way to fund myself.

From January onwards I spent day and night locked away in the back room of my house. I would begin working the moment I woke up until last thing at night. I was off the radar to most of my friends and family. I wanted to give my venture every chance to succeed. I also needed a name for my company. Arena Red was the name I had earmarked while at Rangers. I had written the name down on the back of my rucksack at school and felt this name would come in useful one day. It was too easy, so I began researching company names for weeks. There must be a suitable name for my company. No matter how hard I tried the only name that kept coming into my mind was Arena Red. Eventually I went with my instincts. Some things are just meant to be.

To secure some immediate income I developed a series of partnerships. I targeted those organisations which I could genuinely give back to from my own network of companies. However many of the organisations just agreed to subscribe and I knew they did this to simply support me. In fact they had very little to gain by becoming a partner. David Shortland, a very successful businessman from Coventry who owns Shortland Horne estate agents, was the first to join. No explanation or selling required. He simply said 'I am not sure what the partnership entails but I will do this for you'. I then went to see Peter Dean, the owner of the successful Happy Egg Company. I didn't even need to ask for any support. His words were to the effect that he was not sure how his company would benefit from our partnership but they will never know if they don't support me. What a gentleman and that sums up the calibre of the man. Like David Shortland, Peter was giving me a chance to pursue my ambitions. Meeting Ken Sanker was as surreal. He simply said 'How much do you need? Send the invoice to my P.A.' The meeting was over in five minutes. In all honesty David, Peter and Ken had nothing to gain. Once again this demonstrated the humanity in people to help someone trying to make a go in life.

The support I gained from David, Peter, Ken and many other organisations proved to me compassion exists in society and if you live by integrity somehow you will find doors opening for you when you least expect them to. I genuinely believe I was being watched from above.

It wasn't all plain sailing and I had my challenges as some of the organisations I believed would support me refused to do so. This did knock me, as I had looked after them for several years and went beyond the call of duty on many occasions. It was a learning curve not to take decisions personally. On a salary you have good days and indifferent days. You carry on knowing you will be paid at the end of each month. Being self-employed there was no room for indifferent days. Every day has to count. This itself put a new perspective on my working life.

Still in need of partners, I travelled to Glasgow to meet several of my contacts. At this stage I was apprehensive as many had turned me down. My first meeting was with Stuart from ArchiStarchi. I explained the situation and before I could say anything he said he would take one of the partnerships. Stuart could feel my angst and, even though he was a relatively new business, he did something that will live with me for the rest of my life. I knew he had little money to spare but he gave me the confidence to keep going. Anyone who knows me will tell you I am an emotional character. When Stuart agreed to become a partner anyone in touching distance could feel the relief. It was the boost and confidence I needed. I was back. I will repay him big time one day. Glasgow was a success with Gordon Stewart from SFM and Raj Bains, a local businessman, also putting pen to paper and, with the required partners on board, I could now focus on the website and other important areas.

I very quickly discovered how lonely life can be running your own business. There have been many times when I have sat in bed until the early hours of the morning thinking *what the fuck have I done?* Fear rears its ugly head when you least expect it. It can be relentless and it is so easy to give in to your fears. Then the inner strength of belief, desire, persistence and the reasons why you are following your dream take over and that gives me the courage to continue on the path I have now chosen. I genuinely try and take the positives out of each day and ensure I am working towards my goal. I always believe eventually something positive will transpire. Like most people I have good days, bad days and indifferent days. I can go days if not weeks when things just do not work out for me. It's my coping mechanism that helps me through those challenging times. Over the years I have learned fear keeps you alive and becomes a driver of motivation.

It is early days though I have no doubt the venture will challenge people to change their mindsets to aspire to a better life. I feel I am on the tipping point of something that will be life-changing. The new venture is still in its infancy and Lord knows what's in store, though I will never stop dreaming of my next destination.

EPILOGUE

I have encountered numerous challenges throughout my life and at the football clubs I have worked for. While I always try and maintain a positive outlook, I have also had my fair share of demons to contend with. Certain actions or emotions trigger negative memories from my childhood days, which occasionally conflicts with my state of being. I know I have devalued myself on several occasions, due to the fear of losing what you have. Unconsciously you almost become the subservient employee who is just grateful for the opportunity. Yet deep inside you want to be recognised and rewarded for your ability. It's not an excuse — nobody owes me anything. These are demons I have had to deal with and manage to prove there is a better world out there. And there is a better world out there, where people of all races and backgrounds are willing to offer their support for no personal gain as demonstrated throughout my book. Knowing this, I make a conscious effort to remain positive and be respected for who I am. This is the reason why I regularly write my personal and professional goals and constantly challenge myself without putting limits on what I can accomplish. Life is not easy, and I don't expect it to be, but to give up the fight for what is right is too easy.

As the great Cyrille Regis would always say to me, 'even if I have provided just one building block for a future generation of kids to make a successful career in the commercial world of football then I will have achieved a small but important milestone.'

I am also conscious that I am one of the longest serving Asians in British football and that alone brings a burden of responsibility. Whatever the challenges, I have proved no matter what your colour, ethnicity, background or gender anything is possible.

ACKNOWLEDGEMENTS:

Thank you to all the people that made my dream a reality. My family, friends and all the people I met along the way who believed in me to make me realise anything in life is achievable. Without their support my book would not have been possible.

David Shortland – Shortland Horne, Coventry

Peter Dean – Happy Egg Company

Gordon Stewart – Stewart Financial Management, Glasgow

Cyrille Regis MBE

Stuart Thomson – ArchiStarchi, Glasgow

Ken Sanker – LCV, London

Raj Bains, Glasgow

Geoff Harris – Coventry Plumbing & Heating, Coventry

Ozzie Osmand, Coventry

Kevin Banton – Construction Supplies Hardware Ltd, Burton upon Trent

Rob Ally – XL Motors, Coventry

Eamonn & Ian – Hydraulic Hose & Engineering, Coventry

Anoop Deol – Coventry Road Dental Practice, Bedworth

Tony McGurk – Twincentric, Witney

Derek Bond – Bond Chartered Accountants, Edinburgh

Alex Davis (Publisher & proof reader)

Andy Turner (Coventry telegraph)

Manish Bhasin

Jim Brown – Coventry City FC Historian

Mick Parsons

Andy Moss (A genius who should be on stage)

Kash Taank (Punjabi Glaswegian hospitality at its best)

Baroness Verma

Jeets & Neeta Aulak

Jason Dickens from Jade Studios

Adam Dent and Lee Corden from Advent PR

Printed in Poland
by Amazon Fulfillment
Poland Sp. z o.o., Wrocław

55917028R00154